HOUSE OF GOD

The Historic Churches and Places of Worship of the St. Louis Area

James J. Schild
Introduction by William Barnaby Faherty, S.J.

THE Auto Review

Florissant, Missouri

ii

Printed and bound in The United States of America

Schild, James J.
House Of God - The Historic Churches and Places of Worship of The St. Louis Area

Bibliography:
Includes Index

Library of Congress Catalog Card Number 95-76653
ISBN: 0-9624958-6-7

The Auto Review P.O. Box 510, Florissant, MO 63032

99 98 97 96   9 8 7 6 5 4 3 2

Blessed are they that dwell in thy house O Lord. They
shall praise thee for ever and ever.   Ps 83, 5

Lord, I have loved the habitation of thy house, and the
place where thine honour dwelleth. Ps 26, 8

I have hallowed this temple which you have built and
have put my name here forever. I will constantly watch
over it and rejoice in it.   1 Kings 9, 3

Behold, I build a house to the name of the Lord my God,
to dedicate it to him and to burn before him sweet
incense   2 Chron 2-4

CONTENTS

PREFACE

The concept for this book came to me in the summer of 1990 as I was waiting for a wedding to finish at Holy Trinity Catholic Church. The newly married couple would soon be riding away in our 1929 Cadillac Town Car, but as I watched from the back pew it occurred to me that that few St. Louisians were aware of the interesting, historic churches I have visited over the past ten years. I thought there surely must be at least 100 churches that were old and interesting enough to warrant a book on the subject. I never could have guessed at that time that the number would quickly grow to 272 before the project was completed in the Spring of 1995.

The primary purpose of this book is to document the architecture and the accompanying history of the congregations, churches and places of worship that have caused St. Louis to be called the ecumenical capital of the country. St. Louis is known as an important center for all of the major religious groups and its religious pluralism and ecumenical character are a significant part of the history of the area. This is the first book to recognize this character and bring all of the individual histories into one source. There have been other attempts at presenting this information, but none have achieved the completeness of HOUSE OF GOD. This book is intended not only for the person interested in the religious history of the area, but for the student of the architecture, sociology and art of St. Louis and vicinity.

I realized very early that because of changes in both the buildings and the congregations, the only reasonable way to organize this book was to list the churches in alphabetical order according to the name of the present tenants. This method is refined further in that the present name is used only if the structure is now a church or place of worship. If it is being used for some other purpose, then the name given is that of the most recent use as a place of worship. Each heading page identifies the name of the church, the religion or denomination, the date the

structure was built and the current address. The former name in some cases identifies the previous tenants, while in others, it is the previous name of the same congregation. Beneath that is the listing of any recognition as a historic site. Additionally, all churches and important individuals are noted in the index in the back of the book so that any church past or present may be located easily.

Included in the back of the book is a map showing the general location of the churches so that the reader may find them if so desired and look closer at details impossible to illustrate here. The appendices include a glossary of religious and architectural terms and a section describing the major religions and denominations of the area.

The information presented in this book was gathered using a variety of methods. Some of the churches were identified from previous books or articles, while others were only found by driving the streets of the area. Sometimes, when I would travel to a location to find a church to which I was directed, I would arrive and find more in the same general area. Other churches were found because someone told me that I should look at it. It was a surprise to find how many people had a memory of a particular church that was an important part of their life at some point. Some of my friends directed me to a church that was important to them and gave reasons I should include it in this book.

The photography was a very time consuming project that sometimes took up entire days. On some good days, I could get to as many as ten churches. On other days, I could only do one as things such as lighting direction and weather affected opportunities. In some neighborhoods, I had to deal with harassment and threats from passing cars and from pedestrians which made photography more difficult.

The compilation of information on each of the buildings was the most tedious and time consuming part of the project. In most cases, I sent a simple questionnaire to the church asking for the basic data I needed to tell the story. The response to these questionnaires was very poor even with a follow-up letter. In some cases, the church was contacted with either a phone call or a visit to verify necessary information. It was obvious that some of the congregations did not know the history of the building they occupied. Once this basic level was completed, information was compiled, added and corrected from other sources, including the twenty-seven books and pamphlets listed in the selected bibliography in the back of the book.

The cornerstone, if present, was a starting place for the build date. In some cases the cornerstone reflects the closest date available to when the church was constructed. In North St. Louis, many of the cornerstones have been covered or removed and the information on the buildings now shows only when the present tenants moved in.

In some cases, even the most basic information was not available and I had to spend hours at the libraries, county and city assessor's office and city archives to get the data needed. Sources such as building permits, city and county directories, phone books and church histories were used to make the information as complete as possible. Although the dates reflected in city building permits predates the actual construction in most cases, the date used gives a representation of when the building was erected. Some information was even found in newspaper archives at the St. Louis City Library.

A few of the churches were very helpful and volunteered historical books and literature about their building and congregation. If little or no information is listed under a church, it is because after having exhausted all means, I was not able to find anything on that structure.

When available, the text includes the names of the people who directed the formation of the congregations and the construction of the buildings. When available, the architectural details and construction materials of the structure are noted.

References to local Landmarks and Historic Districts are taken from information provided by the Landmarks Association of St. Louis, Inc.

Recognition of buildings by the National Historic Register is by the United States Department of the Interior. This information is noted according to the latest information available at the time of publication.

I decided that St. Charles, Alton and a few selected churches on the east side would be included because most St. Louisians consider these areas to be part of the Greater St. Louis community. Most importantly, they are a part of the character and history of the area. Plans are already underway for a book on the historic churches of Southern Illinois that will more accurately show that portion of the country.

There were some people who helped me acquire the information for this book and deserve recognition. Gene Boll, one of the Friends of the Shrine of St. Joseph, provided a valuable copy of the 1911 book on Notable Catholic institutions. My wife, Myrna, her mother Ruth Smith and Reverend Dona Tipton encouraged the inclusion of and provided information on some of the Illinois churches.

My gratitude goes out to the people at the office of the St. Louis City Archives who spent time with me finding building permit and block records. I have to thank Larry Hassel who helped with the cover layout. I could not have produced this book without the cooperation of Richard Balducci of Balducci Publications who produced the halftones for reproduction. I am grateful to the researchers who came before me and gathered what information there was on the churches of St. Louis. I am sure there are still churches I have overlooked, but I believe I have included the most important ones. My apologies to the ones I have missed.

I was very fortunate to have Father William B. Faherty create the informative introduction to HOUSE OF GOD that sets the scene for the hundreds of stories contained in this book. His insight into the total picture of the religious history of St. Louis has been a valuable contribution.

James J. Schild 1995

INTRODUCTION

When the visitor at the top of the Gateway Arch looks beyond the immediate tall buildings of the St. Louis business district, he sees an amazing number of churches. A forest of steeples abounds in Soulard on the near southside where eighteen ethnic churches served the needs of immigrants. He looks farther south beyond the single tower of St. Francis de Sales to the twin steeples of St. Anthony on the Meramec Avenue ridge. To the southwest he can make out the towers of Kenrick and Eden seminaries; to the west along Market near the Union Station he gets a glimpse of the south tower of a pre-Civil War church, St. John the Evangelist, and farther on the green dome of the Great Cathedral, barely visible among the apartment houses on Lindell. Then he looks to the near northside where Zion Evangelical Lutheran stands out and Holy Trinity's facade resembles that of the Cathedral of Chartres. Far to the northwest on a clear day he sees the white dome of St. Stanislaus Seminary where the missionary Father De Smet worshipped. Immediately in the downtown area, Christ Church Episcopal Cathedral, right next to the Public Library, hides among the tall buildings. At the foot of the Arch, the Mother Church of the city, the "Old Cathedral," the Basilica of St. Louis, stands alone.

When King Louis XV of France ceded the east bank of the Mississippi to the English in the Peace of Paris of 1763, French residents in Illinois villages chose not to live under the British flag. Many of them moved to Pierre Laclede's new trading post called St. Louis on the west bank of the Mississippi twelve miles below the confluence of the Missouri River. The Illinois French presumed that the west side of the Mississippi would remain under French control. In actuality, King Louis XV had ceded the west bank to his ally Charles III of Spain.

No clergyman came with these Illinois settlers. Occasionally priests from their old villages of Prairie DuRocher, Cahokia and Kaskaskia visited them. They built no church on their arrival even though merchant-trader Laclede

had set aside a block for a church, when he started his post. A Spanish Lieutenant-Governor, Pierre Piernas arrived in 1770 and immediately ordered the townsfolk to erect a temporary log church. Six years later they built a more solid structure on the site of the first.

Father Bernard De Limpach, a member of the Capuchin branch of the Franciscan Order, was pastor of St. Louis from 1776 to 1789. During his 12 years in St. Louis, all residents attended Mass in the log church. Father Bernard baptized 410 white people, 106 Negroes and 92 Native Americans. After he departed, an occasional priest visited the city. The church building deteriorated.

French farmers from Illinois settled in two places not far from St. Louis. Some chose a site along Coldwater Creek twenty miles to the northwest in Florissant Valley. They built a church dedicated to St. Ferdinand on a plot designated by the Spanish commandant. The church records date from 1790 when Father Pierre Joseph Didier, a Benedictine, performed the first Baptism. He regularly served the congregation of St. Charles Borromeo, in St. Charles, Missouri, nine miles away.

French-born Clement DeLor led the other group to a place along the Mississippi six miles south of colonial St. Louis. Originally called DeLor's settlement, it later gained the name Carondelet after the Governor of the Territory. On a hillside overlooking the river DeLor set aside a block for a church and a cemetery. Tradition has it that the villagers built a church there in the late 1700's.

All colonial powers restricted immigration to those of their own established religion. Just as the original settlers in New England were Puritans, those in Virginia Anglicans, and those in New Amsterdam Calvinists, so most of the earlier settlers in French and Spanish colonies were Catholic. Charles Gratiot, a Swiss Calvinist businessman, who married a daughter of Pierre Laclede, was the only prominent Protestant in Creole St. Louis. Under Lieutenant-Governor Zenon Trudeau in the 1790's, many members of other denominations filtered into the area around St. Louis, including the famous pioneer Daniel Boone. But none organized a Protestant congregation.

The Louisiana Purchase brought many English-speaking newcomers mostly from the Middle States along the Atlantic seaboard. Circuit-riding missionaries travelled through the area, but built no churches. Baptist farmers erected the first Protestant Church in the area at Fee Fee and St. Charles Roads northwest of St. Louis in 1815.

Answering a request from local Presbyterians in 1816, the Connecticut Missionary Society sent Salmon Giddings and Timothy Flint to the growing community. The circuit-riding Giddings started the first Presbyterian church west of the Mississippi at Bellvue (later Caledonia, Missouri) eighty miles south of St. Louis and a second one in Bonhomme township west of St. Louis before founding the First Presbyterian Church in St. Louis in 1817 on St. Charles at Fourth Street.

By that time, the St. Louis Catholics had no parish priest. Father Louis Savine, pastor in Cahokia, Illinois, crossed the river for occasional services in the decaying log church.

The Catholic community came alive in 1818 when Louis W.V. Du Bourg, newly consecrated bishop of Louisiana Territory, decided to locate in St. Louis instead of in New Orleans, where earlier bishops had resided. A distinguished educator, seminary director and president of Georgetown College, Du Bourg brought many priests, nuns and brothers from France and Italy to work in parishes and schools. Several of these priests began St. Louis Academy, the forerunner of St. Louis University. When Du Bourg set out to build a brick cathedral, prominent Protestants, in a true ecumenic spirit, joined their Catholic neighbors in contributing to the work. The bishop laid the cornerstone on March 29, 1818.

In July of that same year Du Bourg visited Carondelet and urged the townsfolk to erect a new church on the site designated by Clement DeLor when he laid out the town. Shortly after this, enterprising John Mullanphy gave a thousand dollars to construct a new St. Ferdinand's church in Florissant Valley. This latter was to last longer than Du Bourg's brick structure and remain the oldest church in the Upper Louisiana Territory. A few years later, Du Bourg invited Belgian Jesuits to come west and open a combined Indian school and Jesuit seminary on a fertile plantation three miles to the west.

In the year of Du Bourg's arrival, visiting missionaries John Mason Peck and James E. Welch prodded eleven St. Louis residents to form the first Baptist congregation in St. Louis. Most of the families were black.

The Methodists organized a small congregation in 1822. A prosperous group of Anglo-Americans from Virginia and the Carolinas founded Christ Church Episcopal parish in 1825 with Thomas Horrell the first rector. Several of the founding members had family ties to the wealthy French families.

In the same year (1825) an ex-slave from Virginia, John Berry Meachum, organized a distinct congregation of black Baptists, put up a church on Almond (later Cerre) between Fourth and Fifth, and opened a school.

Bishop Joseph Rosati, a member of the Congregation of the Mission, a Vincentian priest, a recruit of Bishop Du Bourg who had become first bishop of St. Louis in 1826, built a Catholic cathedral of stone to supplant the brick structure on the old church lot between 1832 and 1834. In the following year missionary Bishop Jackson Kemper gave strength to the small Episcopal congregation of St. Louis with a formal visitation.

Up to 1830, the chief newcomers from overseas were Irish. But the writings of a Cologne civil servant, Gottfried Duden, who came to Franklin County, Missouri in the 1820's, brought many Germans to the rich soil of Missouri. Hundreds settled on farms west of St. Louis and thousands located in St. Louis beginning in the mid-1830's.

Many Americans, even amateur historians have tended to divide the German immigrants into two groups; Catholics and Lutherans. Many German Christians, such as the misnamed "Pennsylvania Dutch" and almost all Germans in the English colonies, were members of the

Evangelical Reformed Church. German Catholics were excluded from many English colonies such as Georgia, and few Lutherans came in the colonial period. When German Catholics came to St. Louis in the early days of Missouri's statehood, they found their church solidly established.

Evangelicals came to Missouri from Germany in the early 1830's. Under the leadership of Herman Gerlich, they formed theri first church in the area at Femme Osage in Charles County in 1833. A year later Evangelical Reformed and Lutherans in St. Louis established the German Evangelical Church of the Holy Ghost. The congregation met at Benton School on Sixth between Locust and St. Charles.

A small band of recent arrivals from New England under the leadership of the reverend William Greenleaf Eliot, organized a Unitarian Church in January, 1835 under the name of the First Congregational Society of St. Louis. They met in the Masonic Hall on the northwest corner of Fourth and Pine Streets. When the congregation decided to start a Sunday School, eight teachers appeared, but no students. Two years later the sexton's eight children formed the student body.

A resident of the city, F.W. Southack, recalled the five churches of the city existing in the year 1837: the St. Louis Cathedral on Walnut, the First Presbyterian facing St. Charles at Fourth; Christ Church on Chestnut at the corner of Third; First Methodist at the corner of Fourth Street and Washington Avenue, and the African Baptist Church on Almond between Fourth and Fifth Streets. Three congregation, the Unitarians, the Evangelicals and the Baptist, met in halls not church buildings.

Southack described only two buildings. Christ Church was a "small brick edifice with a cupola in the center." He thought it looked more like an academy than a church. The First Methodist Church was a "plain brick building in traditional Methodist style." (Sharf, History of St. Louis, City and County, p 202)

Lutheran immigrants from Saxony began to worship in the basement of Christ Episcopal Church in 1839. A short time later they built Trinity Church in the 18th block of South Eighth Street and opened a parochial school. The congregation grew strong under the leadership of Reverend C.W.F. Walter. But more of the early Saxon Lutherans lived around Altenberg in the southeast section of Perry County where they opened Concordia Seminary.

In the early 1840's under the leadership of Bishop (soon to be Archbishop) Peter Richard Kenrick, Rosati's successor, five more Catholic churches opened: St. Vincent de Paul at 1408 South Tenth Street, St. Francis Xavier at Ninth and Christy, St. Patrick's at Fifth and Biddle and two for German-speaking immigrants: St. Joseph's at 11th and Biddle Streets and St. Mary of Victories on South Third.

Of these five churches, only St. Vincent de Paul remains in use today. Even though St. Francis Xavier was one of the few buildings in America that won praise from the English novelist Charles Dickens on his American journey, it did not survive the westward movement of the city.

The 1840's saw development and change in other Christian churches. The Evangelical Reformed withdrew from their affiliation with the Lutherans in 1842. Three years later they set up two congregations: a northside church, St. Peter's at Fifteenth and Carr streets, and a southside church, St. Marcus, at Jackson and Soulard, just north of Lafayette Avenue. Eventually the Evangelicals opened the German Protestant Orphan's Home, the Good Samaritan Hospital and a seminary near Femme Osage.

Missouri Episcopalians gained thir own Bishop Cicero Stephens Hawk. He became rector of Christ Church in a new building on 5th and Chestnut in 1844.

Seven families formed the initial local Congregation of the Disciples of Christ under the leadership of Robert Fife. In 1844 Fife appealed to the State Convention meeting in Fayette for funds to erect a frame church. The congregation built at the corner of Sixth and Franklin.

By 1844, the decade when the zealous circuit-riding missionaries brought Methodism to its zenith in the American republic, St. Louis had seven Methodist churches.

In 1850 Concordia Seminary moved from Altenberg, Missouri to South Jeferson Avenue in St. Louis, where a prestigious Lutheran center soon included a church, a high school, a hospital and a publishing center.

Several of the early Protestant leaders, such as Salmon Giddings, had labored under a Congregational-Presbyterian "Plan of Union." This union lasted several decades, until 1852 when members of the Third Presbyterian Church voted to organize a Congregational Church at Sixth and Franklin with Dr. Truman M. Post, pastor of the Third Presbyterian as their leader.

The first Jewish immigrant merchant, Joseph Phillipson, had arrived in St. Louis in 1807. Several others followed, Louis Bomeister, a man of extensive background with a knowledge of seven languages divided his time between St. Louis and Philadelphia where he was president of the synod. While in St. Louis he took the lead in starting the first congregation, the "United Hebrew," in the central city in 1841. In a short time Jews on the southside formed two congregations, B'Nai Brith and Amoona El. These two shortly united as B'Nai El. The first synagogue, a fortress-like octagonal building, opened in the early 1850's at Sixth and Cerre Street. A group of "Reformed Jews" founded Shaare Emeth (Gates of truth) and built a twin-spired synagogue at 17th and Pine. Once spread over the St. Louis area, Jewish families gradually moved toward the central corridor west, where they built many synagogues.

While just one of many ethnic churches on the near southside, St. Joseph Nepomuk at Soulard and Rosati Streets was the first church of Bohemians in America at its start in 1854. Even though far more Bohemian immigrants settled in South Texas, rural Nebraska and the city of Chicago, the St. Louis parish remained the leader of Bohemian cultural life well into the century.

While the original layout of the village of St. Louis was fifteen blocks along the river while only three deep, the predominant trend after the draining of Chouteau Pond in the early 1850's was westward. Many of the early churches in the central area tended to move west.

In 1850, for instance, the Unitarians built a large church at Ninth and Olive. The Disciples of Christ moved to Seventeenth Street and developed a strong religious publishing program. Christ Church Episcopal moved to Fifth and Chestnut and later to 13th and Locust.

By way of contrast, the original French Catholic churches, the Cathedral on the waterfront, St. Ferdinand's in Florissant and the church in Carondelet, by that time called Sts. Mary and Joseph, still stood on the original lots.

The complex issues facing the nation at mid-century split many churches as it did the states. These disputes hurt especially the local Methodist organizations.

The majority of residents of St. Louis in colonial days were people whose French ancestors had lived in Canada or the Illinois country for several generations. Only a few, such as Pierre Laclede himself, were born in France. Few people came directly from France to St. Louis at any time. After the Louisiana Purchase, many Anglo-Americans came to St. Louis. Irish immigrants followed and then an even greater number from the German states, especially the Rhine provinces.

After the Civil War, a "Second Immigration" of people from the east and south of Europe reached America. Only a limited number of these chose to locate in St. Louis in contrast to the great numbers who settled in Chicago, Cleveland, Milwaukee and Pittsburgh. In the St. Louis Catholic community, the Poles opened four churches, the Italians three, the Slovaks, Croatians, Lithuanians, Ruthenians and Lebanese one each.

Immigrants of Orthodox religious background, Greeks, Bulgarians, Serbians, Russians and Romanians, found work in the metro-east industrial areas of Madison, Venice and Granite City. The Bulgarian Orthodox built the first church of their nationally in America in Madison, Illinois in 1907.

Greeks in St. Louis formed a congregation under the direction of Father Pangiotes Phlambolis, a native of Greece. The new congregation rented a former Protestant church at 19th and Morgan (later Delmar) Avenue. The

Greeks built a church on Garrison and St. Louis Avenue on the northside in 1917. Ten years later a terrible tornado reduced it to rubble. After a temporary stay on Kingshighway and Enright, the congregation erected St. Nicholas Church at 4957 Forest Park, just east of Kingshighway.

Eventually the greater St. Louis area would number nine churches of the Eastern Orthodox Christian Federation: three Greek, three Russian, and one each Bulgarian, Serbian and Romanian.

Shortly after the turn of the century warehouses filled the area of the original French village of St. Louis, squeezing the once impressive cathedral and hindering access. The new archbishop John J. Glennon decided to build a new cathedral of Byzantine and Romanesque styles on the northwest corner of Lindell at Newstead. While the basic structure opened for worship in Glennon's Lifetime, artists did not finish the great mosaic art until well into the 1980's. By that time the Catholic community numbered 132 churches. One of the most distinctive was the Lebanese Church of the Maronite Rite at 11th and Chouteau.

In the early 1920's the Metropolitan Church Federation made a study of the city's religious development. Churches reflected other trends in the city. The movement of central city churches to the west end rather than to the north or to the south, for instance, indicated patterns of growth for other institutions such as schools, hospitals, theaters and retail businesses. Washington and St. Louis Universities, Christian Brothers College, Mary Institute, Visitation Academy and Sacred Heart Academy had all moved west. So had many retail businesses and one church congregation after another. The path went straight west to Kingshighway then veered a few blocks to the north of Forest Park and continued west. Northside churches held firm for another twenty years, but the southside churches never wavered. Certain parishes in the central corridor, but juts south of Forest Park, showed marvelous stability: St. Ambrose on "the Hill" and St. James in "Dogtown."

In general, the church authorities did not give much attention to migration trends. When a congregation needed a church and school, the buildings were built, even though demographics might point out that 25 years later no one of that denomination would be living in the area. Ordinarily on moving west Protestant churches kept their original names, such as First Presbyterian now at 7200 Delmar. Catholic congregations, with few exceptions, chose a new saint or patron.

In 1957 the ten Congregationalist and the 49 German Evangelical parishes united to form the United Church of Christ. The union sponsored Eden Theological Seminary in Webster Groves, Deaconess Hospital at Oakland Avenue and Hampton, a home for the aged and one for orphans.

A complex of churches at Union and Delmar give the viewer a chance to view all Greek styles, the Ionic, the Doric, the Corinthian, in one glance. Not one of these churches remains in the hands of the original congregations. While the majority of St. Louis churches follow the Gothic or Romanesque styles, one inner-city church St. Joseph's on Biddle at Eleventh, is in the Baroque style, and two onion domed Orthodox churches reflect eastern Europe, Holy Trinity and St. Michael's at Gravois and Ann. Several are in Federal, or Greek Revival style.

Two St. Louis churches strikingly illustrate the new ultra-style of church architecture: circular St. Anselm's Priory, an awe inspiring temple in West County, and an A-frame church, beautiful St. Mark;s United Methodist Church on Graham Road in Florissant.

The churches of St. Louis display many architectural styles and serve varied patterns of worship.

William B. Faherty, S.J.

William Barnaby Faherty, Jesuit historian and author of twenty four books, has worshiped in ninety three of the churches featured in HOUSE OF GOD. A native of southwest St. Louis, he attended Epiphany Parish School and St. Louis University High School before entering St. Stanislaus Seminary in Florissant in 1931. He finished the long Jesuit course of studies for the priesthood in June, 1944. St. Louis University awarded him a doctorate in History five years later.

After teaching history at Regis College in Denver until 1956, he returned to St. Louis to become Associate Editor of the Queen's Work Magazine. In 1963 the Vice-President of St. Louis University invited him to write the history of the school. He published BETTER THE DREAM on the occasion of the University's sesqui-centennial. In 1972, the history department of the University of Florida recruited him to write the story of man's journey to the moon. The resulting book bore the title MOONPORT. Father Faherty retired from his history professorship at St. Louis University in 1985 and accepted the combined directorships of the Missouri Province Archives in St. Louis and the Museum of Western Jesuit Missions in Hazelwood.

Over the years the Jesuit author has published a thousand articles, six religious tracts, and twenty two other books, most of them on St. Louis subjects. The two most popular are DREAM BY THE RIVER, the story of the local archdiocese and ST. LOUIS: A CONCISE HISTORY, an easy-to-read account of the city from Bellerive to Bosley. The Historical Society of St. Louis County has named an annual award in his honor. MGM adapted his first novel A WALL FOR SAN SEBASTIAN for an Anthony Quinn film (1969)

A fan of the old-time Cardinal champions, of the basketball Billikins, and of the Ambush--several of his former students still play on the team--Father Faherty combines spectating and participating. He skied and ice skated until his eightieth birthday last year, and still plays tennis, swims every day during the summer and hikes along Missouri's great rivers.

ABYSSINIAN BAPTIST

Baptist
1883 (Formerly New Jerusalem Church of the Glorification, Bethany Baptist, Chiesa Diddio Christian Italian Pentecostal, Italian Christian Congregational, Church of God of Prophecy)
2126 St. Louis Ave.
St. Louis, MO 63106

This church, at the corner of Rauschenbach and St. Louis Avenue has had a great number of congregations as tenants in its lifetime. The earliest was noted as the New Jerusalem Church of the Glorification as late as 1929. In 1935, it was the home of Bethany Baptist, but by 1936, it had become the Chiesa Diddio Christian Italian Pentecostal Church. From 1937 to at least 1952 it was the Italian Christian Congregational Church. By 1960, it was the Church of God of Prophecy. The structure is now the home of Abyssinian Baptist Church.

ALL SAINTS

Catholic
1874
7 McMenamy Road
St. Peters, MO 63376

The first group of Catholics in the area of what is now St. Peters met in 1815 in a 35 ft. by 25 ft. log cabin on the east bank of Dardenne Creek. They built their new church on two parcels of land donated by the Bernard, Voisard and Denny families. The original church members were mostly of French and French Canadian descent and named their new church St. Peters. The constant flooding of Dardenne Creek caused them to move to the west bank where a new church was completed by 1834. From 1840 on, the area began to be populated by German immigrants and the church community grew until it was necessary to construct a new building on the site of the present church. In 1856 the name of the parish was changed to All Saints and by 1865 the area began to be called St. Peters instead of Dardenne. In 1874 the growing parish of almost 125 families began construction of the present church. It was completed under the leadership of Father Nicholas Staudinger (1877-1894). The parish was stable until the 1960's when it grew to more than 1500 and to the present with more than 2000 families. The church design is brick neo-gothic.

ALL SAINTS EPISCOPAL

Episcopal
1930
2831 North Kingshighway
St. Louis, MO 63115

All Saints Episcopal Church is occupied by the only black Episcopal congregation of the Episcopal Diocese of Missouri. From 1906 to 1957 the congregation occupied the Former Unitarian Church of the Messiah at Locust and Garrison streets.

ANGELIC TEMPLE OF DELIVERANCE
1907-08 (Formerly Temple Israel)
5001 Washington
St. Louis, MO 63108
City Landmark: January 1972

Temple Israel was founded in 1866 by a group of dissidents from Temple Shaare Emeth. Worship was originally held in Memorial Hall at 19th and Locust and moved later to the Pickwick Theater at Jefferson and Washington. In 1888, a stone temple designed by Grable & Weber was completed at Leffingwell and Pine. In 1907, this structure became the home of the Union Memorial A.M.E. until 1960 when it was finally destroyed for the Mill Creek Valley project. Around the turn of the century, the Temple Israel congregation moved west to the northwest corner of Kingshighway and Washington. The Corinthian order Roman Temple of Caen stone was built in 1907-08 from a design by Barnett, Haynes & Barnett of St. Louis. It is part of the historic Holy Corners District at Washington and Kingshighway in the Central West End of the city. The Temple Israel congregation moved to west St. Louis County in 1964.

ASBURY UNITED METHODIST

United Methodist
1909 (Formerly the Epworth Methodist Church, Chouteau Place ME)
4001 Maffitt Ave.
St. Louis, MO 63113

Asbury was the Edwardsville Mission which started as a Sunday school class in 1914 at the home of Miss Macky a member of Union Memorial on Leffingwell and Pine. In 1918, the Edwardsville Mission united with Bagnell Chapel at 8400 North Broadway under the leadership of Rev. W.W. Goff. The church moved into a store front on the corner of Goode and St. Ferdinand and Mrs. Lilly Holland named the church Asbury after the late Bishop Asbury. The church met there and at another location at Taylor and St. Ferdinand until 1952 when the congregation purchased the present building which had housed the Epworth Methodist Church. The building was designed by Hartshorn - Barber R.B. Co. in 1909.

ASSUMPTION GREEK ORTHODOX
1924(Formerly Assumption Greek Orthodox, First Church of Christ, Scientist)
6900 Delmar Blvd.
University City, MO 63130
National Historic Register
Civic Plaza Historic District

The former First Church of Christ, Scientist was designed by St. Louis architect Thomas P. Barnett. It was built in 1924 as part of E.G. Lewis' plan for the plaza around the lion gates of University City. In 1958, the structure was sold to Assumption Greek Orthodox Church who used it until 1986 when they moved to west St. Louis County. It is now the studio of St. Louis artist Mary Engelbreit.

B'NAI EL TEMPLE

Jewish
1905 (Formerly B'Nai El Temple)
3666 Flad Ave.
St. Louis, MO 63110
National Register, July 21, 1983

United Hebrew was the first Jewish congregation in St. Louis, but in the southern part of the city two new congregations were formed. They were known as B'Nai B'rith and Amoona El. A merger was suggested and the two joined using the first and second names, calling themselves B'Nai El. The B'Nai El Reformed congregation originally met in rooms at Ninth and Lafayette at its founding in 1852 but soon moved to Fifteenth and Walnut. They stayed there until 1875 when they purchased the circa 1867 former Chouteau Avenue Presbyterian Church at the northeast corner of Eleventh and Chouteau. In 1906 they moved to Spring and Flad. The Byzantine-Romanesque temple in red brick was designed by St. Louis architect John L. Wees. After the congregation moved west to Delmar and Clara in 1930, the temple had various uses and tenants including the Compton Heights Christian Church before 1944. The temple was converted to apartments in 1983 by Mead-McClellen and was named Temple Apartments. The B'Nai El congregation is now located in west St. Louis County on Conway Road.

BAIS ABRAHAM CONGREGATION

Jewish
1927 (Formerly University Church of Christ)
6910 Delmar Blvd.
University City, MO 63130

BAPTIST CHURCH OF THE GOOD SHEPHERD

Baptist
1907-08(Formerly Second Baptist)
Kingshighway & Washington
St. Louis, MO 63108
City Landmark: January 1972

The former Second Baptist Church is a Modified North Italian Gothic design made of multi-colored golden brick trimmed in dark red granite, terra-cotta, red tile, and Minnesota sandstone. It was built in 1907-08 from a design by Marian, Russell & Garden, Architects. The original Second Baptist congregation was founded in 1818 as the first Protestant church in St. Louis. It was for many years, the largest Baptist church in the state.

BASILICA OF ST. LOUIS, KING
(The Old Cathedral)

Catholic
1834
209 Walnut Street
St. Louis, MO 63102
National Register
City Landmark: June 1966

The first Catholic church was built on this site in 1770, six years after the founding of the trading post, St. Louis. The original primitive log structure was blessed by Very Reverend Peter Gibault, Vicar General of the Bishop of Quebec. The first church was dedicated on June 24, 1770. This log church soon gave way to a larger building constructed of white oak timbers.. There is no record of this church's dedication, but it was occupied sometime in 1776. This structure served as the cathedral for the installation of Bishop Du Bourg, the Bishop of Louisiana and the Florida. On March 29, 1818 the cornerstone for the first cathedral to be built of brick, was laid by Right Reverend William Louis Valentine Du Bourg, Bishop of New Orleans who had made St. Louis his residence. In January 1819, Very Reverend Felix De Andreis, C.M., Vicar General, blessed the new Pro-Cathedral which had not yet been plastered. The church was 130 feet long, forty feet wide and forty feet high.

In 1826, St. Louis was created an Episcopal See and the Right Reverend Joseph Rosati, C.M. was constituted it's first Bishop. In April of 1830 it was decided that a new cathedral would be built. The specifications were laid by August of that year and it was directed "that the walls should be three feet thick from the foundations to the floor, and two and a half above the floor; the foundation should be sunk four feet in the ground and raised five above the ground; that the church should be eighty by one hundred and thirty, and thirty four feet high from the floor; that the front should be of neat hammered stone, and the sides of good range work." On August 1, 1831, Bishop Rosati laid the cornerstone for the New Cathedral. The church was consecrated on October 26, 1834 and was to be called the Church of St. Louis IX, King of France. The cathedral was designed by architects George Morton and Joseph C. Laveille of St. Louis and is constructed of rubble limestone walls and polished sandstone facade. Its design is Greek Revival with Baroque aspects which are subdued by the earlier removal of six tall stone candelabra which surrounded the parapets flanking the portico. Bishop Du Bourg old brick cathedral, located just to the east of the present structure, burned in 1835. Bishop Rosati obtained from Pope Gregory XVI extraordinary privileges for the cathedral, making it one of the most richly indulgenced churches in the world. The same plenary indulgences imparted to those who visit the seven churches in Rome may be gained by those who devoutly visit the three alters of the Old Cathedral. In 1847, St. Louis was raised to an Archiepiscopal See and Most Reverend Peter Richard Kenrick was created it's first Archbishop.

On October 18, 1914, the title of "Cathedral" ceased when the present New Cathedral on Lindell Blvd. was blessed. On September 20, 1963, after four years of extensive renovation by Murphy and Mackey of St. Louis, it was announced that the church had been decreed a Basilica by Pope John XXIII on January 27, 1961. The church would now be known as the Basilica of St. Louis, an honor which is only bestowed on a few churches in the entire world. The two insignia of a Basilica, the canopeum (umbrella) and tintinnabulum (little bell) are on the right and left, respectively, as you enter the nave. The church stands on the only privately owned ground on the National Jefferson Expansion Memorial site..

BELLEFONTAINE UNITED METHODIST

United Methodist
1855
10600 Bellefontaine Road
St. Louis, MO 63137
St. Louis County Historic Building: July 4, 1976

The original congregation started as a small group of neighbors and friends who met in a newly built cabin in 1805. By 1853, a group of local landowners became interested in building a church on a donated tract of land where the present church now stands. Timber and bricks from the site were used to construct the church which was completed in 1855. The old building still exists on the north side of the new sanctuary which was built in 1965. One of the more prominent members of this church was Helen Lee Richardson. She eventually became principal of McTyeire School in China which was founded by the Southern Methodist Church. During Miss Richardson's term as Principal, the school saw Chaing Kai-Shek and Sun-Yet-Sen as students. Miss Richardson died in China in 1915.

BEREAN SEVENTH DAY ADVENTIST

Seventh Day Adventist
1911 (Formerly Church of the Holy Apostles)
1244 Union Blvd.
St. Louis, MO 63113

The Berean Seventh Day Adventist Church was formed in July of 1904. They met originally at 1208 North Sarah before moving to the former Church of the Holy Apostles at Union and Maple. The structure was built in 1911.

BETHANY LUTHERAN

Lutheran
1928
4100 Natural Bridge
St. Louis, MO 63115

BETHEL EVANGELICAL LUTHERAN

Lutheran
1931
7001 Forsyth Blvd.
Clayton, MO 63105

Bethel Evangelical Lutheran was established in 1913 in Clayton. In 1923 the congregation decided to move to the present location at Forsyth and Big Bend Blvd.. The basement was used for services until the completed church was dedicated in 1934.

BETHLEHEM LUTHERAN

Lutheran
1893-95
2153 Salisbury
St. Louis, MO 63107

Bethlehem Evangelical Lutheran is the oldest Protestant congregation in the Bremen-Hyde Park area. It was organized April 26, 1849 by twelve Lutherans of New Bremen. The first church building was at the southwest corner of North Nineteenth and Salisbury and was dedicated May 5, 1850. This was a small one-story structure in Greek Revival style. A second, larger brick church on the same site was dedicated in 1858. By 1887, construction began on the present church site at the northwest corner of Salisbury and Florissant. The large brick structure was dedicated October 29, 1893, but it was all but destroyed by a fire on January 24, 1894. Rebuilding began immediately and the present edifice was dedicated on April 17, 1895. It is red brick in English Gothic style, traceried windows and buttressed walls and towers. It originally had two spires, with the higher one on the east tower. Both were destroyed in the 1927 tornado. Beginning with the founding of the Ebenezer Lutheran Church in Baden on May 16, 1869, six daughter organizations have been formed from Bethlehem Church.

BLESSED SACRAMENT

Catholic
1907
5017 Northland Avenue
St. Louis, MO 63113

In 1907 a new Catholic parish was organized in the central western section of St. Louis. Father P.H. Bradley, who was charged with this task, found about seventy-five families in the area ready to form the new parish. A suitable site was obtained at Kingshighway Blvd. and Northland Avenue where a neat temporary church was soon built. The present structure was built in 1914.

BONHOMME PRESBYTERIAN

Presbyterian
1841
Conway & White Road
Chesterfield, MO 63017
National Register

This Rural Greek Revival structure is still used for weddings and special events by local residents. The congregation has moved west to 14820 Conway Road. The 1929 Cadillac Town Car is owned by Antique Classic Limousine.

BOSTICK TEMPLE

Church of God in Christ
1925 (Formerly West Park Baptist)
1448 Hodiamont
St. Louis, MO 63112

BOWMAN UNITED METHODIST

United Methodist
1921
4276 Athlone
St. Louis, MO 63115

Bowman was organized in 1879 and its original structure was dedicated in 1881. The church was named in honor of the Bishop Thomas Bowman. After moving to several different locations, the church settled on its present location in North St. Louis. The present building was completed and dedicated May 29, 1921. In June of 1970, the first black pastor, Reverend Aubry Jones reorganized the church and inaugurated new programs and institutions.

CABANNE UNITED METHODIST

United Methodist
1902 (Formerly Cabanne Methodist Episcopal South)
5760 Bartmer Avenue
St. Louis, MO 63112

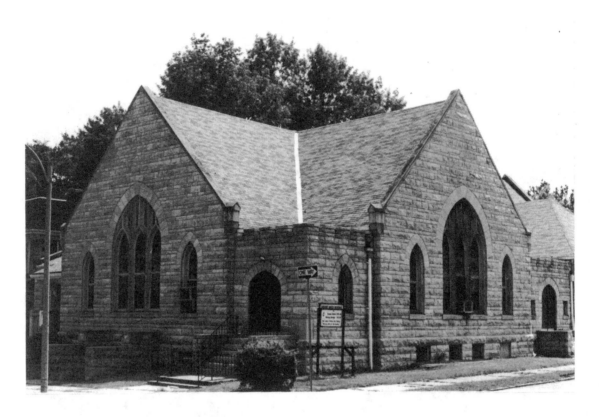

The Cabanne Methodist Episcopal Church began life on November 22, 1896 when forty-two adults and children met in a hall at Goodfellow and Vernon avenues to organize a Sunday school. The congregation worshipped there until August 31, 1902. The site of the present church was acquired in 1901 and the building started that year. The first service in the new church was held November 2, 1902 by Bishop Warren A. Candler. The church from its inception served an all white congregation. When the neighborhoods became integrated during the 1960's non-white members joined the church. At that time, the church became part of the merger between the Methodist Episcopal Church and the South Central Jurisdictional to form the United Methodist Church.

CALVARY CROSS MISSIONARY BAPTIST

Baptist
1896 (Formerly Lutheran Church of Our Redeemer, St. Andrews German Evangelical)
3127 California
St. Louis, MO 63118

This red brick structure was originally built for the Lutheran Church of Our Redeemer in 1896. They moved out in 1908 when their new church on Utah was completed. The church was then occupied by St. Andrews German Evangelical Church which later became a United Church of Christ. The Calvary Cross Missionary Baptist congregation was formed in 1958 and moved into this building in 1964 from their previous location at Chippewa and Iowa.

CARONDELET MARKHAM MEMORIAL PRESBYTERIAN

Presbyterian (USA)
1860-1896
6116 Michigan Ave.
St. Louis, MO 63111
Carondelet Historical Society

In 1845, it was decided that the Carondelet area should have a Presbyterian church, the first Protestant church in Carondelet. The first place of worship for the congregation was a small cabin which stood on the west side of Fourth Street just north of the present church location. On October 28, 1848, the current site at Bowen and Michigan was deeded to the congregation and soon a frame church was constructed. By 1860, it was decided that this building would be replaced with a larger brick church which was completed during the Civil War. By 1896, the congregation had outgrown their brick church and a new large stone church was built adjoining the brick structure. It was designed with rustic stone and Roman style arches.

The Markham Memorial Presbyterian Church was organized in 1901 at 1614 Menard Street in the city of St. Louis. Large scale demolition for the Third Street Expressway in 1958 made a merger with the Carondelet Church necessary

CARONDELET UNITED CHURCH OF CHRIST

United Church of Christ

1870 (Formerly Carondelet Evangelical & Reformed)

7423 Michigan Ave.

St. Louis, MO 63111

The original Carondelet Evangelical & Reformed Church was formed on November 14, 1869. Later, the E & R and the Congregational Churches joined nationally to become the United Church of Christ. The cornerstone for this structure was laid in March of 1870.

CENTENARY UNITED METHODIST CHURCH

United Methodist
1869
55 Plaza Square (16th & Olive)
St. Louis, MO 63103
City Landmark: March 1971

This English Gothic Revival white St. Louis Prairie limestone structure was designed by architects Thomas Dixon of Baltimore and J.B. Legg of St. Louis. The outside trim is of DeSoto stone. The cornerstone was laid May 10, 1869 and the church was dedicated May 28, 1871. The congregation was organized in 1839 and is the oldest Methodist congregation in St. Louis. Centenary is the seat of the Eastern Missouri Diocese of the United Methodist Church and is one of only two original churches remaining in this downtown neighborhood. The church was renovated in 1964 by P. John Hoener & Associates of St. Louis. Centenary serves a local congregation of about 300. It's motto is "Pride in the

Past and Faith in the Future." Centenary has contributed three of its pastors to the Episcopacy to become Bishops. Centenary Church is the resting place of English-born Reverend Thomas Drummond, who was the first Methodist preacher to die in St. Louis. He died in 1835 after being stricken with Cholera. The Drummond tablet in the Pine Street lobby of Centenary was unveiled April 29, 1906. A historical display of the Centenary-St. Louis connection may be viewed in the Eva Tallman Historic Center, directly across from the Bishop's Theater.

CENTENNIAL CHRISTIAN CHURCH

Christian
1896-1904 (Formerly Third Congregational Church)
4950 Fountain Ave.
St. Louis, MO 63113

This Italian Romanesque Revival structure was built during 1896-1904. It was designed by architects Grable, Weber and Groves.

CENTRAL PRESBYTERIAN

Presbyterian
1930
7700 Davis
Clayton , MO 63105

Revival meetings at First Presbyterian Church in 1832 resulted in two colonies being formed, the Des Peres and the Second Church. Six years after the founding of the Second Church, it established a colony of its own, Fourth Presbyterian Church. The Church was formed April 18, 1844 and met at the southeast corner of Sixth and Chestnut streets. In the spring of 1846 the name was changed to Central Presbyterian Church. The church soon purchased a lot on the northwest corner of 8th and Locust streets. The congregation began worshipping in the basement of the building by winter of 1848. The structure, which seated 600, was completed in 1849. By 1870, the congregation had purchased a lot on the northeast corner of Lucas and Garrison avenues and built a chapel. By 1873, the congregation moved to the chapel and the old church was sold. A new building was started and dedication took place on October 1, 1876.

The area around Lucas and Garrison began to change to where the people of the vicinity of Central were not able to support the church. It was decided in 1905 that the church would be sold. The church was to be sold to the Memorial Union Methodist Episcopal, but because it was a black church, the neighboring churches caused the deal to be dropped. Eventually, the building was sold to the Jewish Congregation B'Nai Amoona. Central moved to a new location at the southeast corner of Clara and Delmar where a new church was dedicated on March 15, 1908. By November 1929, declining membership caused the congregation to move again. By March of 1930, a site at Hanley and Davis Drive in Clayton was approved. The cornerstone was laid November 15, 1930 and services opened September 27, 1931. The move also involved a merger with the Clayton Presbyterian Church. The building was designed in the style of an English Country Church of the late 14th Century by architect Charles K. Ramsey.

CHAPEL FOR THE EXCEPTIONAL

Interfaith
1921 (Formerly Winnebago Presbyterian)
3426 Winnebago
St. Louis, MO 63118

This traditional brick structure was built in 1910 with later updates. It was originally the home of the Winnebago Presbyterian Church. The church is now the home of the Chapel for the Exceptional. It is one of the few churches for the handicapped in the nation. The interfaith congregation, led by Reverend Bill Williams, has no formal membership, but serves about 150. They formed in 1972 and were previously located on Hodiamont Avenue in north St. Louis. This facility was occupied in August of 1988.

CHRIST CHURCH CATHEDRAL

Episcopal
1867
1210 Locust Street
St. Louis, MO 63103
City Landmark: July 1966

The congregation of Christ Church was organized in 1819 and met in a house at Second and Walnut. The church was disbanded in 1821 and reorganized in 1825. They met then at a Baptist church until their own building at Third and Chestnut was completed in 1829. The congregation moved again in 1839 to a larger building at Fifth and Chestnut until the present structure was completed in 1867. Building on the present church began in 1859. The Gothic Revival sandstone structure was designed by Leopold Eiditz of New York and was built under the supervision of William John Beattie of St. Louis. The tower was built in 1910. Christ Church became a cathedral in 1888 upon the selection as the seat of Bishop S. Tuttle's Episcopal chair. Remodeling was completed in 1961-63. Emil Frei of St. Louis created the stained glass.

CHRIST CHURCH UNITED CHURCH OF CHRIST
United Church of Christ
1918-1925(Formerly Christ Congregational)
7126 Bruno
Maplewood, MO 63143

Christ Congregational Church was formed July 6, 1890 and originally met at what is now the Shining Light Tabernacle at 7121 Manchester from January, 1891. The present church was started with the basement completed in 1918, followed by the superstructure completed in 1925. A Mr. Koester was the architect of the Modified Gothic stone building. The church has a number of unique features such as the wooden sculpture of the Last Supper sitting on the altar. It was carved by a German craftsman and is four feet long. There are two giant three-panel art glass windows adorning the north & south walls with an additional four art glass scenes appearing on each of the north & south walls. All ten scenes feature Jesus in various stages of his life. These windows were originally contracted in 1925 for a total cost of $500. The Congregational Church became part of the United Church of Christ in 1957.

CHRIST'S SOUTHERN MISSION

Baptist
1921 (Formerly Eden Immanuel Evangelical)
5630 Page Blvd.
St. Louis, MO 63112

CHRISTY MEMORIAL UNITED METHODIST

United Methodist
1914
4601 Morganford Road
St. Louis, MO 63116

In 1892 a physician, Dr. Simmons, held an organizational meeting in Voyce Hall at Morganford Road and Chippewa Street to form a Sunday school, which later grew to become Christy Memorial United Methodist Church. The first small frame church building was erected at Morganford and Beck in 1894 and was known as the Beckville Methodist Episcopal Church, South, later the Oak Hill M.E. Church, South. In 1911 it was decided to move the little frame church from its location to the corner of Morganford and Neosho. At this time the name was changed to Christy Memorial Methodist Church, South, in honor of Calvin Christy, who donated the site of the first church. It was soon apparent that the growing congregation needed a larger building and plans were begun. The present church was completed in 1914 at a cost of $20,000. The first additions were built in 1939 and included a gymnasium and educational rooms. In 1978 the front of the church building was completely remodeled, giving the church a newer, more modern appearance.

CHURCH OF CHRIST HOLINESS

Church of Christ (Holiness) U.S.A.
1906 (Formerly Salem United Methodist)
4301 Page
St. Louis, MO 63113

This was the third location for the Salem Methodist congregation.

CHURCH OF GOD, BADEN

Non-Denominational
1900 (Formerly Baden A.M.E., Corinthian Baptist, Bagnell Methodist)
8373 North Broadway
St. Louis, MO 63147

The building at 8373-75 North Broadway housed several groups beginning in 1900 as the Baden C.M.E. Church. Unitl 1912, it was occupied by the Corinthian Baptist Church and unitl 1920 it was used by Bagnell Methodist. It has been the home of the Church of God since 1925.

CHURCH OF GOD, GRAVOIS AVENUE

Church of God
1886(Formerly St. Lucas Slovak Evangelical & St. Paul Frieden's Evangelical Church)
1222 Allen
St. Louis, MO 63104

The Church of God, Gravois Avenue structure was purchased from the St. Lucas Slovak Lutheran Church in 1960 after they moved to Morganford Road. The church was originally St. Paul Frieden's Evangelical Church and was built in 1886.

CHURCH OF NON-DENOMINATION

Non-Denomination
1909 (Formerly St. Rose Catholic)
Goodfellow & Maple
St. Louis, MO 63112

The St. Rose congregation was formed in 1883 when Father J.J. McGlynn purchased a suitable site at Goodfellow and Etzel avenues in what was then the western part of the city. This group had grown from the small parish served since 1876 dedicated to St. Rosa of Lima. The new church grew at its new location and soon became the most prosperous in the western part of St. Louis. St. Rose became the mother-church of the West End, the parishes of Holy Rosary, St. Mark, St. Edward and others being carved out of it's territory. In 1908 the parish agreed upon the erection of a larger church and Archbishop J.J. Glennon laid the cornerstone on June 27, 1909. This was also the 25th anniversary of the rector J.J. McGlynn. The church was designed by Barnett, Haynes & Barnett, architects.

CHURCH OF ST. LOUIS

Independent
1893 (Formerly Compton Hill Congregational)
3145 Lafayette
St. Louis, MO 63104

The Compton Hill Congregational Church was organized July 3, 1881 under the name Fifth Congregational Church of St. Louis. In 1888, the name was changed to Compton Hill Congregational Church. The cornerstone for this structure, designed by Theodore Link, was laid November 15, 1893. The church was dedicated October 12, 1894. The Church of St. Louis congregation was organized in September of 1943 and previously met at 4200 Blaine Avenue. They moved to this location in 1955. The congregation built a new 3 story school for all grades in 1965 known as the St. Louis Christian Academy. The church serves about 200 members.

CHURCH OF THE MAGDALEN

Catholic
1940
4354 South Kingshighway
St. Louis, MO 63109

The Church honoring St. Mary Magdalen was created when Archbishop John Joseph Glennon, S.T.D. blessed the cornerstone on March 31, 1940

CLAYTON METHODIST

United Methodist
1921
101 North Bemiston
Clayton, MO 63105

The history of the Clayton United Methodist Church goes back to Ralph Clayton, one of the founding fathers of Clayton, Missouri and a dedicated Methodist layman. Mr. Clayton provided a chapel for itinerant Methodist preachers on his farm for services to be held for people of the Clayton area. In 1881 the small group built a church at the corner of Bemiston and Sappington streets and called it Wilson Chapel Church. By 1917 the church voted to build a new building and it was completed in 1922 at the corner of Maryland and Bemiston. In 1960 an education wing was added to the north side of the existing structure providing offices and Sunday school facilities.

CLAYTON MISSIONARY BAPTIST

Baptist
1907 (Formerly Arlington Methodist Episcopal, South)
2801 Union Blvd.
St. Louis, MO 63115

The Clayton Missionary Baptist Church was formed in 1893. They previously met at Forsyth and Skinker Blvd. in Clayton before moving to the present structure in October, 1961. The congregation now numbers 150-175. The building was built by the Arlington Methodist Episcopal, South in 1907.

COLDWATER UNION CHURCH

Various
1851
15245 New Halls Ferry Road
Florissant, MO 63034

This church was built in 1851 from bricks made in a nearby Kiln. It saw use by Baptists, Methodists and Presbyterians on alternating weekends. The building was sold in 1921 for $500 due to non-use and run down condition. From 1925, the building was used as a home by the Patterson Hume family after they sold what is now known as the Deloge Estate of 300 acres. The old church is now the home of V.F.W. Post 4199 and is recognized by the Florissant Historical Society..

CURBY MEMORIAL PRESBYTERIAN

Presbyterian (USA)
1898
2621 Utah
St. Louis, MO 63118

The Curby Memorial Presbyterian Church is the successor to the Westminster Presbyterian Church which began as a mission on October 19, 1873, and was officially organized as a congregation by the Presbytery of St. Louis on December 31, 1873. Soon a lot was purchased on the southeast corner of 18th and Pestalozi streets and the cornerstone of a modest brick edifice was laid on August 10, 1875. For some time services were held in the basement of the new church building. On June 2, 1878, the auditorium was completed and dedicated to Almighty God. Here the Westminster Church held regular services for twenty years.

Early in the 1890's the church purchased the present site at the corner of Utah and Texas streets. In April of 1897, Colonel J.L. Curby made a proposition and a gift of $10,000 to the Westminster Church which led to the erection of the present building. In 1898, the church adopted a constitution and was chartered by the State of Missouri as a corporation under the name of Curby Memorial Presbyterian Church of St. Louis. The Church was named in memory of Miss Joseph Anna Curby, the only daughter of Colonel Curby. The new structure was dedicated on June 26, 1898. At that time, the church had 170 communicant members and 278 students and teachers in Sunday school. On November 5, 1899, Curby Church accepted and assumed full responsibility for the Gravois School Mission, a Sunday school mission located in the vicinity of Arsenal Street and Gravois Road. The architectural design of Old Akron Brick was executed by Weber & Groves of St. Louis. M.W. Muir was the original contractor of the building which has arched wood ceilings of English Gothic design. The round windows are Northern Italian or Romanesque.

DR. FRY MEMORIAL UNITED METHODIST

United Methodist
1892-1905
2501 Clifton
St. Louis, MO 63139

The Clifton Heights Methodist Episcopal Church was founded by a colony of Methodists from the old Union Methodist Episcopal Church and first met under an apple tree where Reverend T.H. Hagerty preached in 1888. Soon after, a small frame church was erected in the valley near Frisco Park between the Frisco and Missouri Pacific Railroad tracks where Scullin Steel now stands. Reverend S.B. Warner formally organized the Clifton Heights Methodist Episcopal Church on November 18, 1892. The congregation soon moved to larger quarters on March 28, 1892. Property was purchased at 2501 Clifton and a new church was built. At this time, the name was changed to Dr. Fry Memorial Methodist Episcopal Church in honor of Dr. Benjamin St. James Fry, then editor of the Central Christian Advocate and the president of the first board of trustees. The new building was dedicated on June 4, 1893 but was destroyed by fire February 16, 1905. The church was soon rebuilt on the site and the new structure was dedicated in May of 1906. The total investment in the new building was $22,190.95.

EASTERN STAR BAPTIST

Baptist
1912 (Formerly Grace Evangelical Lutheran)
3117 St. Louis Ave.
St. Louis, MO 63106

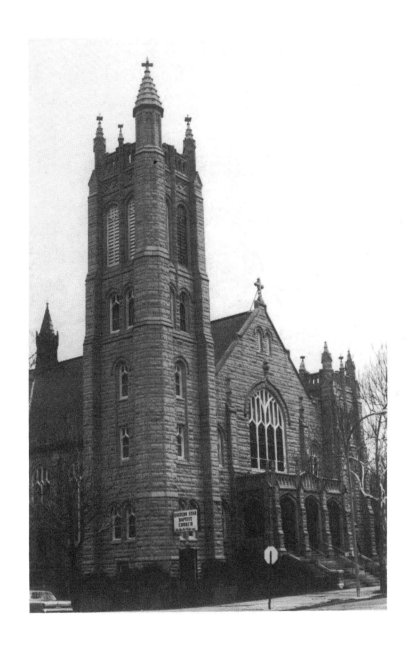

EBENEZER EVANGELICAL LUTHERAN

Lutheran
1922
1011 Theobold
St. Louis, MO 63147

Ebenezer Lutheran was organized in 1869 and this structure was built in 1922.

EDEN UNITED CHURCH OF CHRIST

United Church of Christ
1912 (Formerly Eden Evangelische Kirche)
8930 Eden
St. Louis, MO 63123

Eden was formed as Eden German Evangelical Church which later joined with the Congregational Church nationally to become the United Church of Christ.

EIGHTH CHURCH OF CHRIST, SCIENTIST

Christian Science
1928
Wydown & Skinker
Clayton, MO 63105

In January of 1926, some members of the Fourth Church on Page began discussing the idea of starting another branch. The Eighth Church was formally organized on February 8, 1926 and held the first service two weeks later in Dorr & Zeller Hall at Waterman and Debaliviere. By April 18, 149 Charter Members signed the record of membership. In December of 1926, the lot was acquired for the new church at Skinker and Alexander Drive. The site had been used as a pond for the 1904 World's Fair and the ground was found to be not suitable for the upright structure originally planned. The architectural firm of Aegeter and Bailey of St. Louis designed the Italian Gothic church which would be built by the Humes-Deal Company. Ground was broken July 2, 1928. The church is constructed of stone, brick and terra cotta and has seating for 1000. The first service was held in the new edifice on October 21, 1929. The first service in the auditorium was on November 27, 1930 with formal dedication being March 12, 1944.

ELIOT CHAPEL

Unitarian Universalist Association
1859-60 (Formerly Grace Episcopal)
Taylor & Argonne
Kirkwood, MO 63122
St. Louis County Historic Landmark: 1979

In 1834, a small group of Easterners invited William Greenleaf Eliot to come to St. Louis as it's minister. The congregation first called itself the First Congregational Church of St. Louis. Their second church was built at Olive and Ninth streets in St. Louis. In 1854, they changed the name to the Church of the Messiah. The Church of the Messiah eventually occupied the large church which stood at the corner of Locust and Garrison Avenue. It was designed by Peabody and Stearns of Boston. This was the third building for the Unitarians. From 1906 to 1957, the church was owned by All Saints Episcopal which was the only black congregation of the Episcopal Diocese of Missouri. It was later the home of the First

Cathedral Church of the Apostolic Faith. Although a national and city historic landmark, the building was demolished in 1987 after extensive damage by vagrant's fires. Half of that original congregation left when Eliot spoke out against slavery, but from the group that stayed they went on to accomplish much. This original congregation founded Washington University, The Mary Institute and the Mission Free School and they organized the drives that created the St. Louis Public Schools. A second church was formed in Lafayette Square called the Church of the Unity was started and after some moves both churches joined to form the first Unitarian Church of St. Louis in 1936. Eliot Chapel began as a group of families from the First Unitarian Church living in the southwest St. Louis County area. In spring, 1954, Dr. Thadeus Clark, minister of the First Unitarian School brought a request that the church should become the nucleus of a new church school. Instead, a new church was started and in the fall of 1954, Eliot Chapel began as a branch of the First Unitarian Church of St. Louis. After many moves, the old Grace Episcopal Church at Taylor and Argonne became available in 1961 and it was purchased for $25,000. The structure was designed by R.S. Mitchell and is of Rural Gothic design of limestone. The new church was occupied in 1962. By the early 1970's the old church was restored and renovated as Eliot Chapel grew to over 350 members. A fire April 1, 1977 seriously damaged the church, but it was rebuilt and reopened in 1978. The renovation work later included a new roof, a new spire and restoration of the 130 year old stonework. Emil Frei of St. Louis produced the stained glass.

EMMANUEL EPISCOPAL

Episcopal
1866
9 South Bompart
Webster Groves, MO 63119

Emmanuel Episcopal Church was formed in October, 1867 at the present location, which was on the farm of Mr. & Mrs. Richard Lockwood. The Gothic stone structure was designed by Henry Isaacs and completed in 1867. The original building occupies the space between the crossing and the tower door. The building was updated over the years with final additions being completed in 1965. The pipe organ, part of the 1965 remodeling, is said to be a duplicate of the organ in the Air Force Academy Chapel in Colorado. The bell in the tower was the gift of Mr. & Mrs. Lockwood's daughter Jane. The bell maker misspelled her name Jenne and cast that name into the bell. It is believed to be her height in 1867, as is the cross on the spire. Emil Frei of St. Louis produced stained glass for later remodeling work.

EMMAUS LUTHERAN

Lutheran
1902 (Formerly Emmaus Evangelishe Lutherische Kirche)
2671 Shenandoah
St. Louis, MO 63104

Emmaus Evangelishe Lutherische Kirche was formed in 1901 at about 2300 South Jefferson. The church was designed and built by architect/builder Frederick Bonsack. The white stone, Romanesque Revival structure at South Jefferson and Armand Place was built and occupied in 1902. The church now serves about 140 active members in the south city area.

EPIPHANY UNITED CHURCH OF CHRIST
United Church of Christ
1891 (Formerly Ebenezer Deutsche Evangelische Kirche)
2915 McNair
St. Louis, MO 63118
Benton Park Historical

Epiphany United Church of Christ was formed in 1964 through the merger of the Ebenezer and St. Andrew's congregations. The Ebenezer Evangelical congregation, formed in 1888, has occupied this building since it was built in 1891. The United Church of Christ was formed in 1957. The present site of Epiphany Church was occupied in 1875 by St. Paul's German Methodist Church which was organized in 1874 as a mission of the Eighth Street German Church.

EPIPHANY OF OUR LORD

Catholic
1911
6596 Smiley
St. Louis, MO 63139

Epiphany of Our Lord congregation was formed in February of 1911 in a storefront and soon moved by Father English to a building on Ivanhoe between Bradley and Scanlan. The present church, built by Hof Construction of Basilica brick design was completed February 26, 1911 and occupied in September of that same year.

EPISCOPAL CHURCH OF THE HOLY COMMUNION

Episcopal
1938
7401 Delmar Blvd.
University City, MO 63130

The Epsicopal Church of the Holy Communion was founded in 1865 as a mission Sunday school of Trinity Church. The congregation originally met in a brick school house on Morgan Street near Garrison. In 1869 a lot was purchased at Washington and Ewing which was later exchanged for one at Leffingwell and Washington, where they built a chapel in 1870 and a church in 1877. The Leffingwell and Washington structure is now the home of the Jamison Memorial C.M.E. The Episcopal congregation moved to its new chapel in 1938, meeting in the rear of the present building. The new sanctuary was built in 1950

EVANGELIST CENTER

Church of God In Christ
1900 (Formerly Grace Evangelical Lutheran)
6402-06 Dr. Martin Luther King Blvd.
St. Louis, MO 63133

EVERGREEN OUTREACH CENTER
1897 (Formerly St. Augustine Catholic)
3114 Lismore
St. Louis, MO 63107
National Historic Register: October 2, 1986
City Landmark: March 1986

In 1874 the ecclesiastic authorities decided to erect a German parish in the vicinity of the Old Fairgrounds. In August of that year Reverend Henry Jaegering purchased ground on Hebert and Lismore for the new church. On the first Sunday of October 1874, the cornerstone of the new church and school was laid by Vicar-General Muehlsiepen in honor of St. Augustine. In 1895, the pastor, Reverend Henry Hukestein determined that the parish need a larger facility, so on the first Sunday in May, 1896 Archbishop J.J. Kain laid the cornerstone for the present building. The new church was dedicated on August 29, 1897. The 13th Century Gothic Revival style church was designed by architect Louis Wessbecher of St. Louis. The stained glass windows were by the Emil Frei Art Glass Company.

FEE FEE BAPTIST

Southern Baptist
1870
11330 St. Charles Rock Road
St. Louis, MO 63044

The Fee Fee Baptist congregation was formed in 1807 and met originally at the old meeting house (1828) that now stands at Old St. Charles Rock Road and Fee Fee. This structure of Colonial brick was built in 1870.

FERGUSON UNITED METHODIST

United Methodist
1939
33 South Florissant Road
Ferguson, MO 63135

The Methodist Church of Ferguson began in 1886 in Tiffin Hall with Charles L. Smith preaching and William H. Tiffin as Sunday school superintendent. The first building was erected in 1887 at the northeast corner of Tiffin and Clark on property donated by Mr. Tiffin. Both the original church and the hall are now private residences. By 1912 the church relocated in a new brick building at the present site on property donated by Mr. and Mrs. Louis Maull. This building was destroyed by fire September 4, 1938. A new cornerstone was laid July 22, 1939. The earlier cornerstone was preserved on the west side of the new building, which was completed in 1940. In 1951, a one-story ell was added with a second floor added in 1955.

FIFTH MISSIONARY BAPTIST

Missionary Baptist
1923 (Formerly 6th Church of Christ, Scientist)
3736 Natural Bridge
St. Louis, MO 63107

FIRST BAPTIST

Baptist
1882 (Formerly St. Mark's English Lutheran)
3104 Bell
St. Louis, MO 63107

The oldest of the black Baptist churches in St. Louis is the First Baptist, organized in 1833 after the white congregation of that name became extinct. The congregation was then known as St. Paul's Colored Baptist Church. The first pastor was Reverend Barry Meacham. The first location of First Baptist was on Almond between Fourth and Fifth streets. In 1885 the congregation moved to the former 3rd Baptist building at 1320 Clark Street where it remained until moving to the present building in 1920. The present church was formerly the home of St. Mark's English Lutheran which is now located at 6337 Clayton Road. The sale was confirmed January 31, 1918. The design of the 3104 Bell facility is English Gothic and was designed by architect C.K. Ramsey. The original cornerstone was laid May 29, 1881 and the church completed in October of 1882. The structure suffered a fire in 1942 which gutted it to the walls. It was subsequently rebuilt.

FIRST CHURCH OF CHRIST, SCIENTIST

Christian Science
1903
5000 Westminster
St. Louis, MO 63108
City Landmark: January 1972

The brown brick trimmed limestone Classical Renaissance structure was designed by Marian, Russell & Garden in 1903. This congregation, founded in 1894 was one of the first five Christian Science churches in the world.

FIRST CONGREGATIONAL

United Church of Christ
1900
10 West Lockwood
Webster Groves, MO 63119

FIRST CONGREGATIONAL

Congregational
1901
600 Henry Street
Alton, IL 62002

On June 30, 1870, at the home of Captain and Mrs. F.T. Lewis on Fourth and Henry streets, a meeting was held by those in favor of organizing a Congregational church. They were mostly New Englanders who had been members of the First Presbyterian Church. The first meeting of what was called the Evangelical Congregational Church of Alton was held July 8, 1970. A mission chapel was acquired at Henry Street and Sixth. This was used as the meeting place for the congregation, then called the Church of the Redeemer until 1899, when it was decided that a new church should be built. The groundbreaking was April 1, 1901 and the cornerstone was laid August 14, 1901. The new church was completed and the first service held October 31, 1901. The name was changed June 2, 1965.

FIRST METHODIST

Methodist Episcopal
1831(Formerly First Methodist Episcopal)
617 South Main Street
St. Charles, MO 63301

The First Methodist Church building was built and paid for by Mrs. Catherine Collier in 1829. Mrs. Collier was a devout Methodist and it was not long after her arrival from Philadelphia that she began organizing a church and making plans for the construction of a church building. The first church was a frame building on the north side of Jackson Street between First and Second. For several years, services were held by "Missionary Preachers". Mrs. Collier invited other Protestant groups to use the building for services following the Methodist services. The congregation soon outgrew this building. On October 18, 1831, David Barton and Charles Collier conveyed to Mrs. Catherine Collier a lot of ground now known as 617 South Main Street, upon which a new church building was built for the Methodist congregation. The church was built with double doors to open wide for weddings, funerals and school recitals. The bricks were handmade and the walls were built 18 inches thick. It is believed that this is one of the oldest buildings of any denomination still standing in Missouri. In her will dated August 31, 1833, Mrs. Collier bequeathed the lot of ground with the church to the Methodist Episcopal Society. Mrs. Collier also donated funds to create the Methodist college which was incorporated in 1837 and continued educating ministers on Third street between Jefferson and Washington until 1892. The church building at 617 South Main was used until 1852 when a larger building was necessary. The congregation moved then to Fifth and Clay streets and stayed there until 1896. They moved to Fifth and Washington in 1896. This building burned in 1953 and the congregation had to build a new church at 8th and Clay. In 1963, this congregation joined with the other Methodists in St. Charles and on January 13, 1963, the Faith United Methodist Church came into being at 3232 Droste Road. The old church is now used for offices.

FIRST PRESBYTERIAN

Presbyterian (USA)
1891-97
West 4th & Alby
Alton, IL 62002

First Presbyterian Church in Alton was organized in 1837 and met at Second & Market. The present building of Ashler limestone was designed by architect Theodore Link and was built in 1897. This is the oldest or second oldest church in Alton. Emil Frei of St. Louis producd some new stained glass for the church in 1990.

FIRST PRESBYTERIAN

Presbyterian
1927
7200 Delmar
University City, MO 63130

The First Presbyterian Church, the third Presbyterian congregation west of the Mississippi, was formed in 1817. It is considered to be the mother-church of most of the Presbyterian churches in St. Louis. By 1859, First Presbyterian had moved four blocks west of its original location at Fourth and St. Charles streets. By 1890, the church moved west again, this time by twelve blocks. In 1912, the congregation moved to Sarah and Washington. The present structure at 7200 Delmar was built in 1927 in developer Cyrus Crane Willmore's University Hills subdivision. It is constructed of stone and was designed by architects LaBeaume & Klein.

FIRST UNITARIAN

Unitarian
1905
East 3rd & Alby
Alton, IL 62002

In 1836, the First Unitarian Society of Alton was organized after a series of sermons held by Dr. William Greenleaf Eliot. In 1854 the Society purchased the site of the Catholic church and cathedral, called St. Matthews, that had been partially destroyed by fire in 1854-55. The first Unitarian church was built here as the Catholics had rebuilt on one of the cities opposite hills so that the two locations were thereafter referred to as "Christian Hill" and "Heathen Hill" by the jokers of the city. The new Gothic Revival edifice was designed by Ernest J. Hess. The structure is built of what was called "Bushhammer Alton Limestone." The original cornerstones from the Catholic church may be seen today incorporated into the present building, a bit higher up the front wall. In 1889 the Society was incorporated as the First Unitarian Church of Alton. The present church was built on this site and dedicated July 26, 1905.

FIRST UNITED METHODIST

United Methodist
1915 (Formerly Hagerty Memorial Methodist Episcopal)
600 North Bompart
Webster Groves, MO 63119

On January 3, 1895, a group of people met in the home of Mr. and Mrs. Walter F. Roff and organized the Tuxedo Park Methodist Episcopal Church with eleven charter members. The congregation met in a building at 667 Atlanta until 1910. In 1909 two lots were purchased on the corner of Bompart and Fairview and the old church was sold to a Lutheran group. A basement was dug and the lower level completed by 1910. Ground was broken in 1915 for the new building which was dedicated in 1916. The new church was named the Hagerty Memorial Methodist Episcopal Church after Thomas Hagerty, a former pastor and benefactor. The sanctuary was remodeled in 1956.

FOURTH BAPTIST

Baptist
1929
2901 North 13th
St. Louis, MO 63107

The Fourth Baptist Church was started as a mission of the Second Baptist Church in 1851. A church building at Twelfth between Benton and North Market was dedicated in 1862 and served the congregation until 1929 when the present structure was completed on the same site. The new church was designed by Oliver Tucker and was styled after a small church from 1887.

FRIEDEN'S "PEACE" UNITED CHURCH OF CHRIST

United Church of Christ
1907 (Formerly Friedens Deutche Evangelische Kirche)
1908 Newhouse
St. Louis, MO 63107

Frieden's German Evangelist Church was organized in 1858. The congregation originally met in the Fairmont Presbyterian Church at Ninth and Penrose. The first building on the present site was finished in 1861. It was made of red brick in the Gothic style. The present structure , designed by Otto J. Boehmer in English Gothic Perpendicular style was built in 1907. Its walls are over-sized brick with terra-cotta trim. The interior and stained glass windows were heavily damaged in the 1927 tornado. The church was rebuilt and rededicated in 1928. A new altar and chancel were added in 1932. The corner tower of the church is eighty feet in height.

FULL GOSPEL ASSEMBLY

Apostolic
1870 (Formerly Unitarian Church of the Unity, St. Joseph's Catholic)
2123 Park Avenue
St. Louis, MO 63104

An offshoot of the Unitarian Church of the Messiah was formed in 1868 as the Church of the Unity. A corner lot at Park & Armstrong was purchased and a stone Gothic chapel was dedicated there in 1870. The Church of the Unity remained at this location until 1916 when the building was sold to St. Joseph's Lithuanian Catholic Parish and the Unitarians moved to 5015 Waterman Avenue.

FULL GOSPEL NON-DENOMINATIONAL

Non-Denominational
1883-84 (Formerly Lafayette Park Presbyterian)
1505 Missouri Avenue
St. Louis, MO 63104

The Lafayette Park Presbyterian Church was founded in 1878 as a colony of the Walnut Street Church. Many of the church's members came from the old Chouteau Avenue Church which was disbanded in 1875. This Greek Revival church was built in 1883 from plans by John H. Maurice who along with George I. Barnett designed many of the Second Empire Townhouses in the Lafayette Park district. This church, like many others in the area, was damaged severely by the tornado of 1896. The building was rebuilt after the tornado in its original design in cut stone. Lafayette Park Presbyterian Church occupied the building until 1946 when it merged with the Tyler Place Presbyterian Church.

GALILEE BAPTIST

Baptist
(Formerly First Church of the Nazarene, Delmar Avenue Baptist)
4300 Delmar
St. Louis, MO 63108

The Galilee Missionary Baptist congregation was organized in 1898 and met previously at 2808 Spruce Street. The congregation, which now numbers 425 members moved to the 4300 Delmar location on April 16, 1947. The structure had previously been occupied by the Delmar Avenue Baptist Church and before that the First Church of the Nazarene. The original construction date of this stone building is unknown.

GRACE & PEACE FELLOWSHIP
Presbyterian (PCA)
1906 (Formerly Central Presbyterian, B'Nai El Temple)
5574 Delmar
St. Louis, MO 63112

Central Presbyterian purchased the lot on the southeast corner of Delmar and Clara in September of 1906 for $10,000 and began construction of a new church. The sanctuary was first used for worship on March 15, 1908. The new Hodgman Memorial Organ was dedicated May 24, 1908. By November of 1929, the congregation had decided to move due to declining membership and competition from Westminster Presbyterian at Delmar and Union. On Christmas Eve, 1929, the congregation voted to sell the Clara and Delmar building to the Jewish congregation B'Nai El for $190,000. By March of 1930, the new site at Hanley and Davis Drive in Clayton had been approved, along with a merger with the Clayton Presbyterian Church.

GRACE CHAPEL
1910 (Formerly St. Henry Catholic)
1230 California
St. Louis, MO 63104

On January 16, 1885, Reverend J.A. Hoffman was called upon by the ecclesiastic authorities to organize a new German parish in the south city area east of Grand and south of Chouteau. On March 13th 1885, a tract of land was purchased on California Avenue between Rutger and Hickory streets. The cornerstone was laid on June 28 and the building dedicated September 13th by Vicar-General Henry Muehlsiepen. By 1896 a new, larger church had been decided upon, but the tornado of that year laid the old church to ruins and the decision was confirmed. The plans had to be temporarily abandoned but the cornerstone was finally laid by Archbishop Glennon in May, 1909 for a new church designed by Wessbecher & Hillebrand. The brick & stone Romanesque/Basilica church was dedicated in May of 1910.

GRACE EPISCOPAL

Episcopal
1925(Formerly Grace Episcopal Church)
2600 Hadley
St. Louis, MO 63106

Grace Episcopal started as a small wooden building in 1846. This original structure was torn down in 1881 and enlarged to accommodate 700 people. The congregation became linked with the Holy Cross Mission by Bishop Daniel Tuttle in 1910 when its position was so poor it resigned it's charter. Circle No. 3 of what was then known as Old Village was set aside and the new church of Norman Gothic stone was built in 1925. It is now the home of Grace Hill Settlement House.

GRACE PRESBYTERIAN

Presbyterian
1909
5603 Ridge Avenue
St. Louis, MO 63112

The remains of Grace Presbyterian Church were being pushed over into rubble as this photograph was being made. The cornerstone of this stone church at the corner of Ridge and Hamilton was laid on December 18, 1909. The cornerstone was all that remained in early 1994.

GRACE UNITED METHODIST

United Methodist
1892-1913
6199 Waterman
St. Louis, MO 63112
National Historic Register
City Landmark

In 1886, the Union Methodist Episcopal Church at Garrison and Lucas on Piety Hill decided to move their congregation to a location west of Vandeventer so the Lindell Methodist Church came to be. The structure of English Gothic Bedford stone was designed by Theodore Link of Link, Rosenheim and Ittner and the cornerstone was laid at Lindell & Newstead in 1892. As shifts in population occurred over the next fifteen years, it was decided that the congregation should move again. It was at this time that the decision was made to take the church with them on this move. On March 18, 1913, work began on breaking ground and tearing down. Stone by stone the church was rebuilt at the new location at Skinker and Waterman. It is not an identical church as the top stones became the bottom and the building was built in an opposite direction from the first. At this time the name was changed to Grace Methodist Episcopal Church. Upon the unification of the three branches of Methodism, the word Episcopal was dropped. The new chapel was completed on September 21, 1913 and on October 11, 1914 the church edifice was finished and rededicated.

During the 1960's the membership of the church reached a high of 1800. One of the significant achievements of that period was the formation of the Skinker-DeBaliviere Community Council. In 1975 the sanctuary was redecorated and soon after, the St. Louis Symphony Orchestra began using the facility for chamber music concerts because of its excellent acoustics. The series of windows of the north and south vestibules represent the Saints Matthew, Mark, Luke, John, Peter and Paul.

GRACE UNITED METHODIST

United Methodist
1880
700 Henry Street
Alton, IL 62002

GREATER FAIRFAX BAPTIST

Baptist
1907 (Formerly Bethel Evangelical Church)
2941 Greer
St. Louis, MO 63107

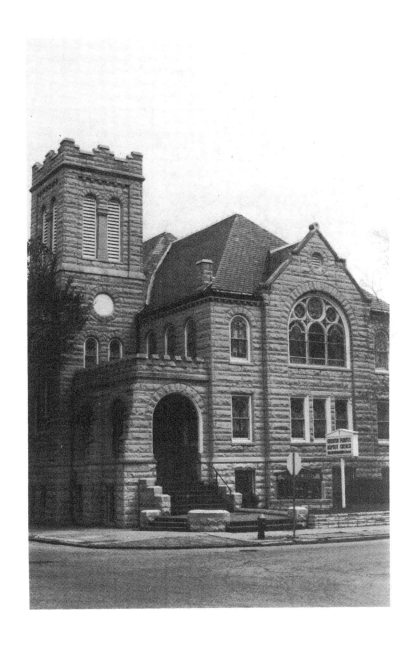

GREELEY PRESBYTERIAN

Presbyterian
1929 (Formerly Greeley Presbyterian)
2240 St. Louis Avenue
St. Louis, MO 63106

The Greeley Presbyterian building now houses the 23rd Street Theater.

HOLY CROSS LUTHERAN

Lutheran (Mo Synod)
1867-1889
2650 Miami
St. Louis, MO 63118

This German Evangelical Lutheran congregation is located at Miami and Ohio in south city. This brick, Gothic Revival/Basilica church was designed by Griesse and Weile of Cleveland. The cornerstone was laid June 16, 1867 with the dedication on December 8, 1867. The structure was fully completed on October 27, 1889. The original 160 foot spire was destroyed in the 1896 tornado and replaced in late Victorian style. In 1905 Theodore Lange gave the congregation a replica of Leonardo DaVinci's "Last Supper" hewn in marble. The altar painting "Christ in Gethsemane" was donated by G. Knoepp to replace "Crucifiction" painted by a student.

HOLY CROSS PARISH

Catholic
1909
8115 Church Road
St. Louis, MO 63147

The roots of Holy Cross Parish go back to 1863 when a small house at the northern boundary of Calvary Cemetery served as the summer residence of Archbishop P.R. Kenrick. Reverend Soligne lived here and arranged a small room as a private chapel where the local German and French Catholics met for mass. Reverend Casper Doebbner, rector of Holy Trinity Parish soon obtained permission of the Archbishop to found a new parish in this, the most northern suburb of St. Louis. The cornerstone was laid by Father Doebbner in Summer, 1863 and the new church dedicated on May 3, 1864. The present church was dedicated May 23, 1909. In 1873 the English speaking parishioners separated and organized Mount Carmel as a new parish further north. In the 1860's, a mission of the church was formed in Spanish Lake.

HOLY FAMILY

Catholic
1799
116 Church
Cahokia, IL 62206
National Historic Register: 1970
St. Clair County Historical Landmark: 1964
Catholic Daughters of America: 1924

On October 21, 1698, the tour began which was to result in the founding of Cahokia, the first permanent settlement in the Mississippi Valley. On May 1, 1698, the Bishop of Quebec granted to the Seminary of Foreign Missions the right to establish missions on both banks of the Mississippi river for its entire length. On July 14, 1698, Reverend Francis Jolliet de Montigny was chosen Superior of the expedition and Jean Francois Buisson se St. Cosme, Antoine Davion, and Thaumur dit La Source were named to accompany him.

On Easter Monday, 1699, Montigny's party. thirty strong, left Chicago for the lower missions. In the meantime, St. Cosme had started building and May 14, 1699 had a presbytery built and timbers cut for the chapel. The chapel was completed and the Mission of the Holy Cross was formally established 14-22 May, 1699. This original structure was replaced by a new church built in 1787. Regulations of the church wardens established Holy Family September 24, 1799 at the present site. These regulations were approved by Vicar-General J. Fr. Rivet and by X. Joseph, Bishop of St. Louis, January 29, 1832.

HOLY FAMILY CHAPEL

Catholic
1899
Sisters of St. Joseph of Carondelet
6400 Michigan Avenue
St. Louis, MO 63111
National Historic Register: February 28, 1980
City Landmark: November 1974

The first Sisters of St. Joseph of Carondelet came from Lyons, France in 1836 at the request of Bishop Rosati. A convent school was opened that year. Two more sisters, trained in teaching of the deaf-mute arrived in 1837 and the St. Joseph School for the Deaf was opened in the same year. In 1840, the Sisters of St. Joseph started St. Joseph Academy. In 1899, the cornerstone of the Holy Family Chapel was laid by the Gillick Brothers Construction Company. Aloyisius F. Gillick was the architect. The Romanesque style structure with rounded domes and roof was completed the same year. Schrader and Conradi, St. Louis sculptors, provided the Italian Marble altars and the marble communion railing. Joseph Sibbel of New York was commissioned to create the Holy Family group on the main altar, the angels, apostles and stations of the cross. The stained glass windows in the sanctuary and main chapel were done by the Wallis Company of St. Louis. The organ was from Kilgen & Sons of St. Louis.

HOLY FAMILY

Catholic
1925
4125 Humphrey
St. Louis, MO 63116

In 1898, the Diocese of St. Louis decided that it was necessary to establish another German-speaking parish south of Tower Grove Park. The new parish was formed November 6, 1898 out of parts of St. Anthony, St. Francis de Sales and St. Aloyisius parishes. Charged with the organization, Reverend John F. Reuther of Creve Coeur acquired a beautiful site, consisting of the entire block at Oak Hill and Humphrey Streets. The cornerstone for the first temporary structure was laid August 20, 1899 by Vicar-General Henry Muehlsiepen. The upper story of this first church was completed in 1907. By 1910, the parish numbered 150 families. The growth of the parish required the construction of the present church, which was built in 1925.

HOLY ROSARY

Catholic
1922
4325 Margaretta
St. Louis, MO 63115

The Holy Rosary parish was founded in 1891 by Reverend D. J. Lavery and a beautiful red brick church was soon built at Margaretta and Newstead. By 1910, the parish numbered 250 families and was already outgrowing this structure and ground was purchased for the new building adjacent to the original church. The cornerstone for the new white stone church was laid November 19, 1922.

HOLY TRINITY SERBIAN EASTERN ORTHODOX

Eastern Orthodox
1928
1910 McNair Avenue
St. Louis, MO 63104

HOLY TRINITY SLOVAK
1896 (Formerly Holy Trinity Slovak, St. Paul's Evangelical)
1808 South Ninth
St. Louis, MO 63104

St. Paul's Evangelical Church was built on this site in 1896, replacing an earlier structure built in the 1860's and destroyed by the 1896 tornado. In 1924 it became the Most Trinity Slovak Catholic Church which was closed in 1984 due to the urban flight. Holy Trinity was organized in 1893 and had previously occupied an old Baptist church at Twelfth and Park which was dedicated by Bishop J.J. Kain in 1898. That church was demolished for the widening of Twelfth Street in 1924. The church was desanctified in 1989, restored, and is the now the home of the Ninth Street Abbey, a restaurant.

HOUSE OF DELIVERANCE

Pentecostal
1906 (Formerly Second German Evangelical)
1524 East Grand
St. Louis, MO 63107

IMMACULATE CONCEPTION

Catholic
1935
2934 Marshall
Maplewood, MO 63143

The rapidly growing suburb of Maplewood made the organization of a Catholic church in this residential district a necessity. In 1904, Reverend D.W. Clarke, assistant at St. Teresa's, was charged by the archbishop with the founding of this new parish. A brick, combination building used for church and school purposes was built and a congregation of over one hundred families was gathered within its walls. In 1935, the present red brick church was dedicated.

IMMACULATE CONCEPTION-ST. HENRY

Catholic
1908
3120 Lafayette Avenue
St. Louis, MO 63104

The first church of the Immaculate Conception was dedicated in the St. Louis Archdiocese in 1854 by Archbishop Kenrick. The date was September 10, a full three months before Pope Pius IX declared the Dogma of the Immaculate Conception. The church stood at Eighth and Chestnut and its first pastor was James Duggan who was later named Vicar-General of the Archdiocese of St. Louis, Coadjutor to Archbishop Kenrick, Bishop of Antigone, and finally Bishop of Chicago. In 1870, the first church was abandoned and the parish was dispersed. Reverend Patrick O'Reilly secured a new location and a second church opened its doors in 1874 at Jefferson and Lucas.

During the time of O'Reilly, two other parishes of note had their beginnings, St. Kevin's in 1876 at

Compton and Rutger and St. Henry's in 1885. The 1896 tornado leveled the first Church of St. Henry and was replaced with the new church at Rutger and California in 1910. St. Kevin's became the leading English speaking parish in the south side.

In 1904 ground was broken for a new church for St. Kevin replacing the second one at Park and Cardinal. The old church was decided to be inadequate for the needs of the parish and it was decided to move south to Lafayette Avenue and Longfellow Blvd. The church was designed by architects Barnett, Haynes, & Barnett. The new Gothic edifice was dedicated in honor of the Immaculate Conception of the Blessed Virgin Mary, December 19, 1908, by Archbishop J.J. Glennon. It would be known as Immaculate Conception-St. Kevin's Parish.

In 1969, St. Henry's church was closed by the Archbishop and in 1977, St. Henry's was merged with Immaculate Conception and the church was known as Immaculate Conception-St. Henry's.

IMMANUEL LUTHERAN

Lutheran
1867
115 South 6th
St. Charles, MO 63301

IMMANUEL LUTHERAN

Lutheran (ELCA)
1928
3540 Marcus Avenue
St. Louis, MO 63115

Immanuel Lutheran was organized in February of 1847 and met at 15th and Delmar. This is the second Lutheran congregation in St. Louis and the oldest Central States Synod/ELCA congregation. The congregation was organized by Reverend J.F. Buenger who was also the founder of Lutheran Hospital and the Lutheran Family and Children's Services. The present building was constructed on the grounds of the Western Evangelical Lutheran Cemetery. The groundbreaking was August 28, 1927 and the cornerstone was laid November 13, 1927. The English Gothic brick church was designed by Ewald Froese and was dedicated in the fall of 1928.

IMMANUEL UNITED CHURCH OF CHRIST

United Church of Christ
1929 (Formerly Immanuel Evangelical)
126 Church Street
Ferguson, MO 63135

Immanuel Evangelical Church was organized in 1888 at the present location in Ferguson. In its 107 years of service, there have been 12 persons enter the ordained ministry from Immanuel Church. In 1957 the Evangelical Church became part of the United Church of Christ. Immanuel now has almost 1000 members.

IMMANUEL UNITED METHODIST

United Methodist
1927
2105 McCausland
St. Louis, MO 63143

Immanuel Methodist Episcopal South Church was organized in May, 1888. The area around Immanuel Church was known as Benton. Houses were far apart, streets were unpaved and the only means of transportation to the city of St. Louis was the daily local train that stopped at the old Benton Station just east of Ecoff Avenue. A group of local commuters on that train felt that the community needed a Methodist church. The Methodists in that area would catch a train to Union Station, then at 12th and Poplar, then walk or take a cab to Centenary Methodist at 16th and Pine. The first place of worship was in a small frame hall on the southwest corner of Bruno and Forest Avenues. A new frame church was erected on the southwest corner of Blendon Place and Bruno Avenue, under the direction of Reverend J.D. Vincel, the first pastor of the congregation. Until the dedication of the church, it was known only as Benton Methodist Church. At the dedication ceremony in 1890, the church was officially named, Immanuel Methodist Episcopal Church.

The lot on Blendon and Bruno was sold and the church was moved to 2115 McCausland Avenue, the present site of the church parking lot. The cornerstone for the present church was laid on Sunday, June 11, 1927. The first worship was January 18, 1928. The structure was valued at $85,000. In 1954, the front of the sanctuary was remodeled and the entire worship center was rebuilt at a cost of $17,000. Fourteen members of Immanuel have been ordained into the ministry.

JAMISON MEMORIAL C.M.E.

Christian Methodist Episcopal
1876 (Formerly Episcopal Church of The Holy Communion)
609 North Leffingwell
St. Louis, MO 63103

The Jamison Memorial C.M.E. Church was founded in 1917 by the Reverend Nathaniel Moore at South 23rd and Adams streets. It was named in honor of Bishop Monroe Franklin Jamison. The congregation later moved to locations at 3144 Laclede, 400 South Jefferson and 413 South Jefferson. On October 22, 1945, Reverend Charles A. Craig moved the congregation to the present location at Leffingwell and Washington Avenues. The structure had previously been the home of the Episcopal Church of the Holy Communion. That congregation had built a previous church on this same site in 1870. Throughout the years, the church was renovated and improved and the mortgage was paid off by June, 1983. The congregation has 968 members at this time. The original cornerstone of the church has been destroyed.

JESUS UNITED CHURCH OF CHRIST

United Church of Christ
1896 (Formerly Jesus Evangelical)
1115 Victor
St. Louis, MO 63104

On November 2, 1894, some former members of St. Mark's Evangelical Church, then at Soulard and Third streets organized a new congregation, Jesus Evangelical Church. The group met at Soulard Market Hall and occupied a church at Twelfth and Victor. The present church site was purchased on April 2, 1895. The current edifice with Gothic tracery and blue rose window was dedicated on March 8, 1896. In 1913, Jesus Church merged with St. Paul's Friedens Church in their building at Thirteenth and Allen and sold the previous structure to St. Lucas Slovak Lutheran Church.

KENNERLY TEMPLE

Church of God in Christ
1929
4307 Kennerly
St. Louis, MO 63113

KINGSHIGHWAY UNITED METHODIST

United Methodist
1926 (Formerly Carondelet Methodist Episcopal)
900 Bellerive Blvd.
St. Louis, MO 63111

The Kingshighway United Methodist Church came into existence as an organized part of the Methodist Episcopal Church in the fall of 1877. It was named the Carondelet Methodist Episcopal Church and met at the Marketplace of Carondelet , Market House Square on South Broadway. This is between the present Courtios and Schirmer Streets. The first church building was erected on the southeast corner of 2nd and Union streets, now Pennsylvania Avenue. It was a small frame building with clapboard sides, referred to as the "Cracker Box" by neighbors. A modern brick church was erected on the southeast corner of Blow Street and Virginia Avenue in 1890. This building is now a Nazarene Church.

In 1914, it was decided to move the church to the southwest corner of Kingshighway, Southeast Blvd. and Colorado Avenue, the present location of the church. A small temporary structure was built and the name was changed to Kingshighway Methodist Episcopal Church. In 1915 a brick chapel was built which now serves as the education building. On Saturday afternoon, December 5, 1925, the cornerstone of the present sanctuary was laid. It was dedicated on Sunday, June 13, 1926.

LADUE CHAPEL

Presbyterian (USA)
1948
9450 Clayton Road
St. Louis, MO 63124

In 1941 Mr. and Mrs. Woodson K. Woods circulated the petition, which was presented to the presbytery in December of 1942, requesting the establishment of a church in the Ladue area. The group first met at the chapel at Mary Institute on Warson Road. The organization service was held on November 7, 1943 and Ladue Chapel was officially launched.   The congregation searched for a building site and, in September of 1944, purchased the former home of U.S. Senator George H. Williams on four acres on Clayton Road. In October, 1948, the cornerstone for the new sanctuary was laid. The "Opening of the Doors" dedication ceremony was held on November 13, 1949 at 3:30 p.m.   The structure is Georgian Colonial red brick. Extensive expansion is being completed during 1994-95.

LAFAYETTE PARK BAPTIST

Baptist
1888-1896
1710 Mississippi
St. Louis, MO 63104

The Lafayette Park Baptist Church was originally the Park Avenue Baptist Church, founded in 1867 in a store at Seventh and Chouteau. In 1868 it moved to Park Avenue near Twelfth Street. Due to an increase in membership, the church moved to a new site a the southeast corner of Mississippi and Lafayette. The present name was adopted when the new church was occupied. The church was badly damaged in the May, 1896 tornado, but by late 1896 the church was rebuilt on the same site, at the rear of the lot facing Lafayette Avenue. In 1923 an annex was added with the entrance on Mississippi Avenue. In 1926, the church was enlarged again to accommodate its increased membership. By 1933, the church had 1300 members with 1400 enrolled in the Sunday school.

LAFAYETTE PARK UMC

United Methodist
1900
2300 Lafayette
St. Louis, MO 63104
National Historic Register District: June 28, 1972 & July 24, 1986
City Landmark District: June 30, 1972

A church known as Wesley Chapel was formed in 1843 and was located on Paul Street north of Hickory. The church moved in 1848 to the northeast corner of Eighth and Chouteau. This church was destroyed in a storm while under construction but was rebuilt by 1850. The building was replaced by a larger building in 1873 and the name changed to Chouteau Avenue Methodist Church, South. The congregation moved again in 1888 to Missouri and Lafayette and adopted the present name. The church was badly damaged in the 1896 tornado and later rebuilt. The present structure, fronting on Lafayette Avenue, was designed by Theodore C. Link and was dedicated in 1900.

LANE TABERNACLE C.M.E.
Christian Methodist Episcopal
Pre-1910 (Formerly First United Presbyterian)
910 North Newstead
St. Louis, MO 63108

The First United Presbyterian Church originated in 1839 from a meeting of Scottish families in Downtown St. Louis. The congregation occupied this building until about 1922 when it was taken over by the Lane Tabernacle C.M.E. The Lane Tabernacle Methodist Episcopal (Colored) had previously been located at 4371 Enright, which is one block from the present church. The original cornerstone has been covered.

CHURCH OF THE LITTLE FLOWER

Catholic
1946-49
1264 Arch Terrace
St. Louis, MO 63117

The Church of the Little Flower congregation was organized in 1925. The present structure of modified French Gothic design by Harry I. Hellmuth was completed in 1949. The circular design is representative of the Shrine of the Little Flower in Royal Oak Michigan. The Church of the Little Flower presently serves about 600 families.

LIVELY STONE CHURCH OF GOD

Church of God
1909-1917 (Formerly Evangelische St. Petri (St. Peters) 1843)
4015 St. Louis Avenue
St. Louis, MO 63107

LIVELY STONE CHURCH OF GOD

Church of God
1917 (Formerly North Presbyterian 1845)
3969 St. Louis Avenue
St. Louis, MO 63107

MANCHESTER UNITED METHODIST

United Methodist
1856
129 Woods Mill Road
Manchester, MO 63011
Manchester Historic
D.A.R. Historic
St. Louis County Historic
National Historic Register

Manchester United Methodist Church traces its history back to the earliest days of Methodism in the St. Louis area. By the mid 1820's, a small group Methodists were meeting wherever they could as a circuit rider would visit the community. John Ball, for whom the town of Ballwin was named, responded to the needs of a church by donating a carding machine house, refinishing it and presenting it to the Manchester congregation for use as a house of worship. In 1839, a frame church building was dedicated on the site of today's church complex. That building was later replaced with the brick chapel presently standing facing Woods Mill Road constructed in 1856. The chapel was remodeled and restored in 1959. In 1983, the new larger 10,000 square foot addition was started in addition to more parking space.

Manchester has grown to be the largest United Methodist Church in Missouri with over 3000 members and a staff of nineteen full and part-time workers.

MAPLEWOOD BAPTIST

Baptist (Southern)
1926
7303 Marietta
Maplewood, MO 63143

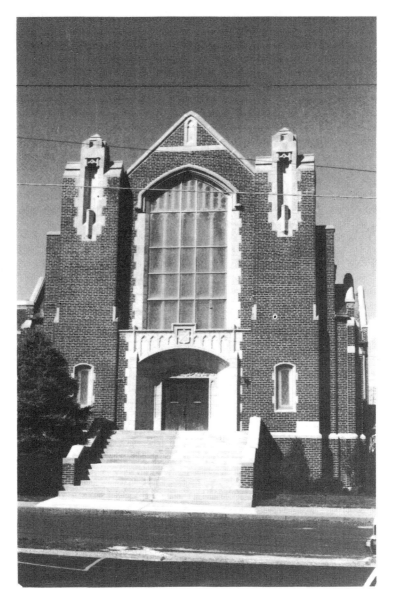

On November 12, 1892 Maplewood Baptist Church was organized. The congregation met at Marshall's Hall at Sutton and Manchester. In the fall of 1894, a lot at the corner of Marshall and Marietta was purchased for $400 and a one room 24' x 40' chapel was built by Sidney Wise. The cornerstone of the first building was laid November 3, 1894. In June of 1903 the building was enlarged by additions to the front and rear and in 1904 and 1905 served as a temporary home for the Maplewood Methodists, whose church had been destroyed. The cornerstone for the present brick building was laid in 1926, but the $85,000 edifice was not ready until late 1927. It was dedicated the first Sunday of 1928. By 1930, the church had 518 members. Maplewood Baptist Church serves about 800 members today.

MAPLEWOOD UNITED METHODIST

United Methodist
1915 (Formerly First Methodist Episcopal)
7415 Flora Avenue
Maplewood, MO 63143

The Maplewood Methodist Episcopal Church had its beginnings in January of 1902 on the second floor of a dance hall known as May's Hall, west of the Maplewood Loop. The church used this facility while the money was being raised to build a church on the present site. In July, 1904, May's Hall burned down, but a tent was erected and the church continued to have services on that location. A brick veneer building was built in 1905, but that was also destroyed by fire in 1914. In 1915, a temporary tabernacle was built at Flora and Sutton. This was used until the present church was completed in 1926. In 1955, an education building was built at a cost of $100,000 and dedicated February 2, 1967.

MELLOW MEMORIAL METHODIST

United Methodist
1904 (Formerly Carondelet Methodist, South, Haven Street Methodist)
6701 Virginia
St. Louis, MO 63111

On May 17, 1857, a brick church was dedicated in the south city area. The pastor was a former circuit rider, Reverend O.H. Duggins who succeeded in raising funds from wealthy Methodists such as Richard Scruggs. In 1904 a new $22,000 building was erected including the bricks from the original building. The names of the church have changed through the years from the Carondelet Methodist Episcopal, South to 1920 when the name became the Haven Street Methodist. In 1941, the name became Mellow Memorial Methodist Church from the Thomas Mellow family who were distinguished laymen in the church and the state. Thomas Mellow came here from Cromwell, England. At least eight members of this church have become ministers and professors.

MEMORIAL BAPTIST

Baptist
1916 (Formerly Anabhangige Evangelical Protestant Kirche)
4001 Fair Avenue
St. Louis, MO 63115

The cornerstone for this German Evangelical Church was laid October 14, 1916. The Memorial Baptist congregation was organized June 2, 1931. The new stone was laid by the Antioch Missionary Baptist Association on June 7, 1959. The church is located directly across from Fairgrounds Park

MEMORIAL BOULEVARD CHRISTIAN

Christian
1917 (Formerly Kingshighway Christian, Hammett Place Christian)
3000 North Kingshighway
St. Louis, MO 63115

Apparently, the Hammett Place Christian Church was derived from the Second Christian Church which was formed in 1889. The Hammett Place Church became the Kingshighway Christian Church, which became the Memorial Boulevard Christian Church. The name Memorial Boulevard came from the memorials that once stood in the wide center ground between the lanes of North Kingshighway north of 5001.

MEMORIAL PRESBYTERIAN

Presbyterian (PCA)
1926
201 South Skinker Blvd.
St. Louis, MO 63105

In July, 1816, the Reverend Salmon Giddings administered the Lord's Supper to a small nucleus of the future First Church, the first known instance of Presbyterians west of the Mississippi celebrating communion. In November of 1817, Rev. Giddings organized the First Church of St. Louis with nine members. As early as 1859, Second Presbyterian Church had determined to establish a new congregation in the western part of St. Louis. On July 4, 1864, a colony of 149 members from Second Church organized the Sixteenth Street Church, commonly known as the Walnut Street Church. In 1878, approximately 100 members of Walnut Street Church living in the southwestern part of the city formed the Lafayette Park Church, merging with the Chouteau Avenue Church, which also had its origins in the Second Church. The central and western residents moved early in 1879 to Washington and Compton avenues and changed the name of the church to match the location.

By 1926, the population of St. Louis had moved steadily west and a new church at Wydown and Skinker was built on the site of the 1904 World's Fair U.S. life saving exhibit. The first service in what was called Memorial Presbyterian was held June 13, 1926. In December of 1931, the sanctuary was completed. Designed in early English Gothic style with outer walls of native limestone, the auditorium is lighted by stained glass windows. In 1975, Memorial Presbyterian merged with the members of Kingsland Presbyterian Church.

MESSIAH LUTHERAN

Lutheran
1929
2846 South Grand Blvd.
St. Louis, MO 63118

The Evangelical Lutheran Church of the Messiah was dedicated December 1, 1929 under the direction of William F. Wilk, pastor. The Gothic brick structure was designed by architects LeBeaume & Klein (Louis La Beaume, F.A.I.A.). The congregation was organized March 13, 1908 at the same location. The church today serves almost 600 members.

METRO CHRISTIAN CENTER
1926(Formerly 5th Church of Christ, Scientist)
3452 Potomac
St. Louis, MO 63118

METROPOLITAN COMMUNITY CHURCH

Metropolitan Community
1872 (Formerly St. John's Episcopal, St. Mary's Assumption Ruthenian Greek)
1120 Dolman
St. Louis, MO 63104

The first Protestant Episcopal church in south St. Louis was organized in 1841 on the upper floor of the fire house on Second Street near Plum. Soon, a brick church was built at Fifth and Spruce which was soon replaced by another at Sixth and Spruce in 1853. This property was sold to an Italian Catholic congregation in 1871 and a new church, known as St. John's Episcopal was built on the northeast corner of Hickory and Dolman. After some structural problems, the church, designed by architect F.W. Raeder, was completed in 1872 and consecrated in 1889. The original brick and stone edifice was damaged severely in the 1896 tornado but was soon rebuilt saving only the alter and chancel from the old structure. This church served the congregation until 1903 when they moved to the building now located on Arsenal just west of Grand. The church on Dolman Street was then occupied by a Greek Ruthenian Church called St. Mary's Assumption.

The Catholics of the Greek Ruthenian rite of St. Louis were organized as a congregation in 1905 and worshipped for a while in the chapel of St. John Nepomuk Church. In 1908, the congregation purchased the St. John's Episcopal Church for $10,000 and the name of the parish, which had been founded as St. Andrew's, was changed to St. Mary's Assumption. By 1910, the parish numbered about 100 families. These people were Austro-Galicians. The services were conducted in the Ruthenian language and the Greek Ruthenian rite was employed. The church is now the home of the Metropolitan Community Church.

METROPOLITAN UNITED METHODIST

United Methodist
1904 (Formerly First Methodist Episcopal)
1 East Sixth Street
Alton, IL 62002

The First Methodist Episcopal Church of Alton was organized in 1829. The frist church building was erected in 1834 at 4th and Belle streets in Alton. In 1857, both the church and parsonage burned to the ground. Immediately after, a brick church and parsonage were erected at the corner of Sixth and Market streets. The present church of Mount Holly white brick and stone was built in 1904 at the same location. The structure was designed by L. Pfeiffenberger & Son. In 1970, St. Mark's and First Methodist merged and the name was changed to Metropolitan United Methodist Church. The church serves about 200 members.

METROPOLITAN ZION A.M.E.
African Methodist Episcopal
1882 (Formerly Union Methodist)
613 Garrison
St. Louis, MO 63107

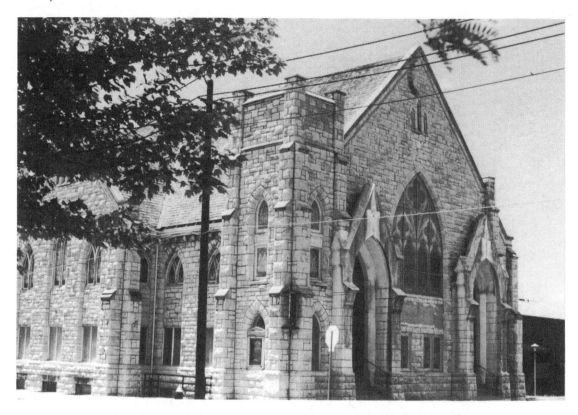

One of the seven churches located in a portion of Stoddard's Addition known as "Piety Hill" was the Union Methodist Church. This stone building on the southwest corner of Garrison and Lucas was built in 1882. Union Methodist was an outgrowth of Ebenezer Chapel, which was St. Louis' first Methodist church. The original church disbanded in 1861 because of the northern sympathy of its members. The church was re-organized in 1862 as the Union Methodist Church and moved into the former Union Presbyterian church at 11th and Locust. The building on Garrison Avenue was destroyed by fire in 1911. The church was rebuilt, but in 1915, the congregation moved into the old First Congregational church at 3610 Grandel Square. The Garrison Avenue structure is now the home of the Metropolitan Zion A.M.E., Church which was formed in 1878.

MIZPAH PRESBYTERIAN

Presbyterian (USA)
1869
11339 St. Charles Rock Road
St. Louis, MO 63044

The Mizpah congregation was organized at the old meeting house on Fee Fee Road on April 16, 1843. For 29 years, the meeting house was shared with the Baptist and Methodist congregations. The Baptists had the 2nd and 4th Sundays, and the Presbyterians on the 1st and 3rd. The present brick, Romanesque Revival structure was built in 1869.

MOUNT GRACE CHAPEL

Catholic
1928
1438 East Warne Avenue
St. Louis, MO 63107

The founding of Mount Grace is an interesting account of the evident steerings of Divine Providence. Mrs. Theresa Backer Kulage manifested her great love and esteem for the priesthood and her love for the Eucharistic Savior by donating the ground and building a chapel for the convent of the Sisters of Perpetual Adoration. Groundbreaking for the convent and chapel was held on May 4, 1927 on the Kulage property overlooking the Mississippi River Valley of north St. Louis across from O'Fallon Park. On the feast of Christ the King, October 30, 1927, Archbishop John Joseph Glennon laid the cornerstone of the new convent. For her charity, Mrs. Kulage was presented the order of the Dames of the Holy Sepulchre by Pope Pius X. The consecration of the chapel alter also presented by Mrs. Kulage was accomplished

February 2, 1929. Mrs. Kulage died on February 25, 1934 after a brief illness. The Convent of Mount Grace is the home of the Sisters of Perpetual Adoration, a Cloistered order known as "the Pink Sisters." The order was established by Arnold Janssen, S.V.D. on December 8, 1896. His desire was to introduce perpetual adoration of the Blessed Sacrament. He chose the "pentecostal" color of the habit, rose colored dress with white veil and white scapular, to remind the Sisters of their obligation to honor God the Holy Spirit and to draw down his divine fire of love upon the cold heathen world. Arnold Janssen died in 1909, his cloistered foundation still in early development. Emil Frei of St. Louis produced the stained glass for the chapel.

MOUNT PLEASANT BAPTIST

Baptist
1932 (Formerly Lutheran Church of Our Savior)
2854 Abner Place
St. Louis, MO 63120

MOUNT TABOR UNITED CHURCH OF CHRIST
United Church of Christ
1949
6520 Arsenal
St. Louis, MO 63139

NATIONAL MEMORIAL FAMILY COGIC
Church of God in Christ
1891 (Formerly 1st Society of New Jerusalem)
620 North Spring
St. Louis, MO 63108

The New Jerusalem Society, also known as Swedenborgians was formed in St. Louis in 1842. They originally met at a chapel on Lucas near Ewing from 1878 to 1891. At that time, they moved to the church at 620 North Spring Avenue, which was known as Cabanne Street at that time. The building is now occupied by the National Memorial Church of God in Christ.

NEW COTE BRILLIANTE CHURCH OF GOD

Church of God
1918 (Formerly Delmar Baptist)
6195 Washington Blvd.
St. Louis, MO 63112

NEW HARMONY GENERAL BAPTIST

Baptist
1886 (Formerly Fourth Christian)
5101 Penrose
St. Louis, MO 63107

This small frame structure, built in 1886, was originally the home of the Fourth Christian Church. It has been remodeled over the years but the original style is still visible.

NEW HOLY TRINITY

Catholic
1899
3519 North 11th Street
St. Louis, MO 63107
City Landmark: April 1979

The eye of the traveler approaching St. Louis from the north either by river or by road, is inadvertently turned to the magnificent church with its two lofty Gothic spires in the northern part of the city. It is the Church of the Holy Trinity, the third church erected there since its organization in 1848. At that time, that part of St. Louis was outside the city limits and known as the suburb of Bremen. The German Catholics of Bremen originally attended St. Joseph's Shrine on 11th and Biddle under great difficulties. In the early part of 1848 Bishop Kenrick sanctioned the establishment of a new German parish. The local landowners, Messrs. Mallinkrodt and Farrar donated sufficient ground at Fourteenth and Mallinkrodt Streets. The cornerstone was laid in Autumn, 1848 and the church was dedicated in honor of the Holy Trinity by Bishop Kenrick on Trinity Sunday the following year. In 1856 the building of a larger church became necessary and a new cornerstone was laid May 18, 1856. That new church was dedicated November 28, 1858.

At a meeting held May 22, 1897, it was decided that it was necessary to construct another larger church. The cornerstone was laid by Archbishop Kain on May 15, 1898 amid a concourse of 25,000 people. The new church was dedicated October 22, 1899 on the fiftieth anniversary of the founding of the congregation. The church, of Late French Gothic design which was modeled after the Cathedral in Cologne, Germany, was designed by Swiss-born architect Joseph Conradi. The solid limestone for the church came from Bedford, Indiana. The towers are 215 feet high. A tornado ripped through St. Louis on September 27, 1927 and severely damaged the back of the church. It was rebuilt without a large octagonal crossing tower that originally stood on the center of the roof.

NEW HOPE OF FAITH TEMPLE

Pentecostal
1894 (Formerly Hyde Park Congregational)
1501 Bremen
St. Louis, MO 63107

The Hyde Park Congregational Church was organized in 1881 and built this Romanesque style church at Blair and Bremen in 1894. At one time it housed the New Shiloh Baptist congregation, but it is now the home of a Pentecostal church. The original cornerstone has been covered.

NEW JERUSALEM CATHEDRAL

Church of God in Christ
1916 (Formerly Holy Name Catholic)
2047 East Grand
St. Louis, MO 63107

The mother-church of the northwestern part of St. Louis used to be the Holy Name Parish, situated near the old water tower. Organized in 1865, it became one of the most prosperous parishes in the city by 1910. The church was originally a brick structure that had been built on what was known as the "College Farm" because the few buildings were occupied in the summer by students and scholastics from St. Louis University, then at Ninth and Washington. Holy name was considered a very cosmopolitan church with families from distinctly varied ethnic backgrounds. On March 26, 1916, the cornerstone was laid for the present church. The building is now occupied by the New Jerusalem Cathedral Church of God in Christ.

NEW PARADISE MISSIONARY BAPTIST

Missionary Baptist
1911 (Formerly 3rd Church of Christ, Scientist)
3524 Russell
St. Louis, MO 63104

Christian
1931
Holly Hills & Tennessee
St. Louis, MO 63111

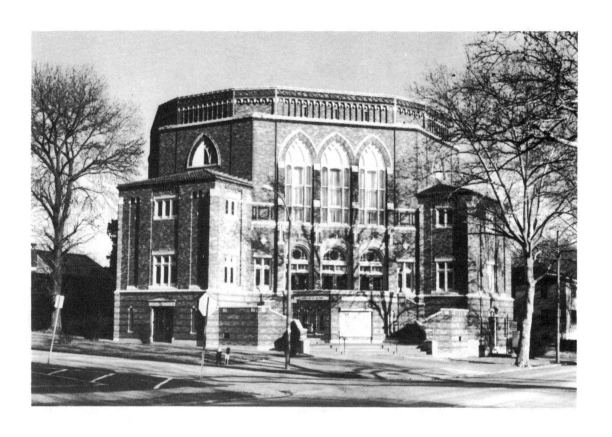

NEW WHITE STONE MISSIONARY BAPTIST

Missionary Baptist
1913 (Formerly Mt. Calvary Evangelical Lutheran U.A.C.)
1444 Union Blvd.
St. Louis, MO 63113

NORTHERN MISSIONARY BAPTIST

Missionary Baptist
1914 (Formerly Bethany Evangelical Congregation)
4449 Red Bud
St. Louis, MO 63115

Bethany Evangelical Church was formed in 1867. The Evangelical Church, later Evangelical & Reformed, became part of the United Church of Christ in 1957. The Bethany congregation moved and became the Bethany-Peace United Church of Christ in Spanish Lake.

OAK HILL PRESBYTERIAN

Presbyterian (USA)
1919
4111 Connecticut
St. Louis, MO 63116

Oak Hill Presbyterian was organized April 16, 1895 and first met in a frame building built on a lot donated by Lucy Bent Russell. That first church was destroyed by fire on March 17, 1907 and the congregation had to meet in rented halls for a while. The first church on the present site was a tent erected in 1908 to be used for summer services. The two story chapel was completed in 1911 and served the congregation until the main church, designed by architects William Green and William Elias was completed in 1919. Additions to the church were made in 1941. Oak Hill Presbyterian serves about 215 members.

OLD DES PERES PRESBYTERIAN

Presbyterian
1833-34
Geyer Road
Frontenac, MO 63131
National Historic Register
D.A.R. Historic site

The Old Des Peres Meeting House is recognized as one of the oldest churches west of the Mississippi River. The Des Peres Presbyterian Church was founded in 1833. The burial grounds to the south of the church holds the remains of early settlers and founders of the church. In the southeast corner of the cemetery are the graves of slaves which are unmarked. In 1983, a stone was set in their memory. The Des Peres Presbyterian Church congregation now meets on Clayton Road at Faith Des Peres Church.

OLD FEE FEE MEETING HOUSE
Baptist, Methodist, Presbyterian
1828-29
Fee Fee & St. Charles Rock Road
St. Louis, MO 63044

The Old Fee Fee Meeting house was built in 1828 and was used as a place of worship for three local congregations; the Baptist, Presbyterians and Methodists. It was used by the Fee Fee Baptist Church for 41 years and is the oldest house of worship in St. Louis County.

OPEN DOOR HOUSE OF PRAYER

Non-Denominational
1904 (Formerly Catholic Church of the Nativity)
5501 Oriole
St. Louis, MO 63120

In the extreme western part of the city (Walnut Park), a new parish, dedicated to the Nativity of Our Lord, was founded in 1905, by Reverend J.C. Granville. A handsome brick church was built and the parish grew very rapidly. The rector of the parish also served as the Chaplain of Calvary Cemetery

OUR LADY OF LOURDES

Catholic
1919
7148 Forsyth
Clayton, MO 63105

Our Lady of Lourdes Parish began on May 7, 1916 with the first mass of Father Francis J. O'Conner in the little stucco chapel that he erected at his own expense just east of the present rectory. A year and a half later on October 14, 1917 Archbishop John J. Glennon laid the cornerstone for the permanent church and then returned to dedicate it on October 26, 1919. The architects Study, Farrar and McMahon received immediate acclaim for the detail and excellence of their Norman-Gothic design. Father O'Conner was designated a monsignor by Pope Pius XII in 1946 and died two years later at the age of 87.

OUR LADY OF MT. CARMEL

Catholic
1938
8747 Annetta
Baden, MO 63147

The parish of Our Lady of Mount Carmel was the most north of St. Louis. From 1863 to 1872 this territory was part of Holy Cross Parish. In 1872, the English speaking members of Holy Cross determined to separate from it and build a church of their own. The first church was at Halls Ferry and Church Road. In 1938, the present church of Bedford stone in Romanesque design was built. In June of 1993, the parish closed and merged with Holy Cross again and was renamed Our Lady of the Holy Cross.

OUR REDEEMER EVANGELICAL LUTHERAN

Lutheran (Mo Synod)
1908
2817 Utah
St. Louis, MO 63118

The Lutheran Church of Our Redeemer congregation was formed March 13, 1894 at the original church located at California and Juniata Streets. Our Redeemer was the first English Lutheran congregation in south St. Louis. The present steel frame and red brick church was built in 1908 and occupied in May of that year. The church was the site of the English Lutheran Synod Convention at which it was decided to join the Missouri Synod. The meeting was held concurrently at Holy Cross Lutheran on Miami. Our Redeemer was also the site of the first Conference for Institutional Chaplains of the LCMS. Our Redeemer was the home congregation of St. Louis Mayor Henry Kiel.

PARKWAY UNITED CHURCH OF CHRIST

United Church of Christ
1871 (Formerly Zion Evangelical & Reformed (Deutch Evangelical))
2801 North Ballas
Des Peres, MO 63131

The Zion Deutsch Evangelical Kirche was formed in 1838 and this Romanesque Revival red brick church was built in 1871. This congregation used the building until 1938 when the new church was built across the road. The old church is now used by the La Iglesia Del Pueblo United Church of Christ.

PARRISH TEMPLE
Christian Methodist Episcopal
1907 (Formerly Unitarian Church of the Messiah)
800 Union Blvd.
St. Louis, MO 63108

This structure was designed by John Marian of Marian, Russell & Garden and is built in Gothic Revival style of hydraulic press brick and stone. It was purchased by the Parrish Temple in 1953.

PENTECOST SAINTS TABERNACLE

Pentecost
1912 (Formerly Markus Evangelical Lutheran U.A.C.)
Angelica & 22nd Street
St. Louis, MO 63107

Markus Evangelical Lutheran was organized in 1904 as a daughter church of Bethlehem Lutheran, its building in Gothic Revival style was completed in 1912. The church is now the home of The Pentecost Saints Tabernacle.

PENTECOST TEMPLE COGIC

Church of God in Christ
1941 (Formerly Notre Dame Catholic Church)
1701 Kienlen
St. Louis, MO 63133

PETERS MEMORIAL PRESBYTERIAN

Presbyterian (USA)
1931
3100 Sidney Street
St. Louis, MO 63104

The congregation of Peters Memorial Presbyterian Church was organized in 1847 at a residence at Thirteenth Street and Park Avenue. They met at homes until 1863 when a church was organized by the Presbytery. It was called the First German Church and met at the old Second Church at Fifth and Walnut. In 1867, a chapel was built at the corner of Tenth and Rutger streets joined by a church in 1871. This structure was destroyed in the 1896 tornado but was rebuilt. A new church was built in 1913 at Sidney and Minnesota and the old church became the Tenth Street Mission. A new church was built in 1931. The congregation originated when a small group of immigrant Dutch held services downtown in a frame building. Later, the congregation was dominated by German and Swiss immigrants.

PILGRIM CONGREGATIONAL

United Church of Christ
1906-7
826 Union
St. Louis, MO 63108
City Landmark: November 1974

The Pilgrim Congregational church was designed by architects Marian, Russell & Gardens and built of pink granite in Modified Romanesque Revival style. It was built in 1906-07. The adjoining chapel, built in 1940 is of matching pink granite in Tudor Gothic Revival style. In 1957, the Congregational Church became part of the United Church of Christ.

PLEASANT GREEN BAPTIST

Baptist
1924 (Formerly Shaare Zedek Jewish)
4570 Page
St. Louis, MO 63113

This building was the home of the Shaare Zedek Jewish congregation. The back section of the building was the home of the West End Page Jewish Educational Center. The cornerstone for that facility was laid March 16, 1924.

PRINCE OF PEACE EPISCOPAL

Episcopal
1916 (Formerly Presbyterian chapel)
8449 Halls Ferry
St. Louis, MO 63147

Sister Miriam of the Episcopalian Good Shepherd Sisterhood came to Baden after the closing of the Bishop Robertson School in 1915. She organized a mission which met in vacant store rooms and eventually in the former Presbyterian chapel at 8449 Halls Ferry Road. The Prince of Peace congregation was organized in 1916 and soon purchased the chapel for their own use.

QUINN CHAPEL A.M.E.

African Methodist Episcopal
1882
227 Bowen Street
St. Louis, MO 63111
National Historic Register: October 16, 1974

The Quinn Chapel A.M.E. Congregation was founded June 25, 1882. The red brick building was originally designed to be a public market in City of Carondelet. The building was sold by the city of St. Louis in the early 1880's for $600 to the African Methodist congregation. The entrance tower was a 1900 addition to house the church bell received as a gift to the church. The church is named in honor of William Paul Quinn, the first black Methodist bishop, who preached in Missouri and opened the west to African Evangelism.

RESURRECTION LUTHERAN

Lutheran
1939 (Formerly Pilgrim Lutheran)
4112 West Florissant
St. Louis, MO 63115

RICHARD M. SCRUGGS MEMORIAL

United Methodist
1929
3646 Fairview Avenue
St. Louis, MO 63116

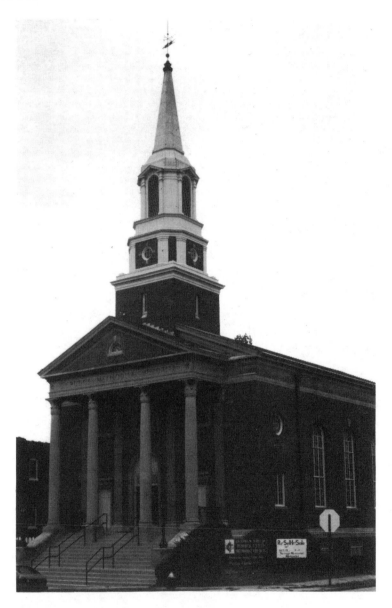

The Richard M. Scruggs United Methodist Church draws its roots from two earlier congregations. The direct ancestor of the church dates from early in the 20th century, when a committee was established to form a Methodist church in the vicinity of Tower Grove Park. On March 16, 1905, this committee purchased a lot on the northeast corner of Grand and Connecticut. On May 18 of the same year, Samuel Cupples bought the adjoining lot and presented it to the church. Soon, a building no longer being used by a nearby Congregationalist church was bought and moved to the site. In 1909, the congregation was legally incorporated as the Grand Avenue Methodist Episcopal Church, South. This served as a temporary structure until a new building replaced it in April, 1910. By the late 1920's, the congregation had outgrown its church and the noise on Grand Avenue was distracting. It was decided to locate a new site and construct a new building.

The other congregation important to Scruggs Church needs to be mentioned here. In 1875, a mission Sunday school was started by Nathan Coleman, a member of St. John's Methodist Episcopal Church South. A church was organized with only six members in 1877. In 1879 another member of St. John's congregation, Richard M. Scruggs, transferred membership to this new church. Richard Scruggs was a businessman who served as Superintendent of the Sunday school until his death in 1904.

When the congregation needed a larger structure for worship, they raised $35,000 by subscriptions. Richard M. Scruggs matched that amount as a gift. The new church was erected at the corner of Cook and Spring Avenues and was named Cook Avenue Methodist Episcopal Church, South. The Quarterly Conference of 1907 changed the name to Scruggs Memorial Methodist Episcopal Church, South. By the late 1920's, the neighborhood was changing and the church was sold to the African Methodist Episcopal Church with the stipulation that when the money was reinvested in a church, that church must carry the name of Richard M. Scruggs. The church Extension Society decided that the money would be allocated to the erection of the new Grand Avenue congregation's structure. Thus the new name for the new church in south St. Louis.

The congregation under the new name of Richard M. Scruggs built a modified colonial style church on the southwest corner of Grace and Fairview for approximately $150,000. The structure was unique to the area in the fact that 27 inches of poured concrete supports the sanctuary floor so that no supports obstruct the view or use of the social hall below.

The Scruggs congregation has suffered from the movement to the suburbs. The church has failed to grow and has been in slow decline. In 1984, the church became a part of the South City Parish, made up of six congregations. Services will be shared with one pastor serving as preacher for services at Scruggs and also at Christy Memorial UMC.

RIVER OF LIFE REVIVALS

Methodist
1892-96 (Formerly Bethlehem Memorial Methodist Episcopal)
2157 South Jefferson
St. Louis, MO 63104

The original church was destroyed by the tornado on May 27, 1896 and this structure was rebuilt in its place.

ROCK HILL PRESBYTERIAN

Presbyterian (USA)
1935
9407 Manchester Road
St. Louis, MO 63119

The Rock Hill Presbyterian Church was organized March 2, 1845 with eight charter members. The site was donated by J.C. Marshall. This structure was built in 1935. The Rock Hill Presbyterian site is recognized as that of one of the oldest churches west of the Mississippi River.

SACRED HEART

Catholic
1907
10 Ann Avenue
Valley Park, MO 63088

On November 14, 1903, Reverend H.S. Kister, senior assistant at St. Liborius, was appointed as rector of Sacred Heart Parish at Valley Park. Previous to that time Valley Park had been attached as a mission to Manchester. On the first Sunday in Advent (November 20, 1903) the first mass was celebrated in the hall. On January 24, 1904, the Valley Park Land Company donated a lot for a church on the condition that the church would be erected within a year. A temporary church was blessed October 23, 1904. The cornerstone for the new church was laid by Archbishop John J. Glennon on September 1, 1907. The structure, designed by Wessbecher and Hillebrand, was dedicated July 4, 1909 by Vicar-General O.J.S. Hoog. The Church is of Germanic-Romanic style. Stained glass is by Emil Frei of St. Louis.

SACRED HEART

Catholic
1893
751 North Jefferson Street
Florissant, MO 63031
National Historic Register

Sacred Heart Parish was organized June 3, 1866 by German speaking Catholics of Florissant. The first church on this site was built in October, 1867. The present structure was dedicated in November of 1893. The stained glass has been replaced by Emil Frei of St. Louis. Sacred Heart now serves about 1400 families in the Florissant area.

SAINT AGATHA

Catholic
1885
3239 South Ninth Street
St. Louis, MO 63118
City Landmark

It was decided in 1871 to establish a new German parish in south St. Louis due to the rapid growth of Saint Peter & Paul. Vicar-General Henry Muehlsiepen laid the cornerstone on October 29, 1871. The new church was dedicated in honor of St. Agatha by Bishop Ryan on July 14, 1872. On April 27, 1884, the congregation, under the leadership of Reverend Henry Schrage, decided to erect a new church which was dedicated by Bishop Joseph Rademacher of Nashville, Tennessee in 1885. The old church was remodeled and used as a school. A transept, sacristy and sanctuary were added in 1899 to the Gothic Revival church which made it one of the most beautiful in St. Louis. Stained glass is by Emil Frei of St. Louis. The church now serves about 285 families and conducts a Latin "Tridentine" mass every Sunday.

SAINT AGNES

Catholic
1890
1933 Sidney
St. Louis, MO 63104

St. Agnes Parish was organized in 1890 by Reverend C.P. Smith. The cornerstone for the new church was laid September 28, 1890 by Very Reverend Philip P. Brady, Vicar-Bishop. The structure is red brick in Renaissance style with a double tower. St. Agnes was originally planned to replace the older Church of the Assumption at Eighth and Sidney which was to move westward. The new church was dedicated on December 6, 1891, but did not replace the Assumption Parish as Archbishop Kenrick had changed his mind about abandoning the older church. The church was renovated in the 1920's.

SAINT ALOYSIUS GONZAGA

Catholic
1925
5608 North Magnolia
St. Louis, MO 63139

On March 9, 1892 Msgr. Muehlsiepen, Vicar-General, offered the first mass of the new St. Aloysius Gonzaga Parish. A temporary church was started on August 16, 1892 at January and North Magnolia. It was dedicated October 16, 1892. The cornerstone for the second church was laid on May 7, 1898 and the church blessed July 17, 1899. Growth of the parish brought the need for a new building and the cornerstone for the present church was laid by Archbishop Glennon on May 3, 1925. The doors opened for the first time for Christmas Mass in 1925. The church was formally dedicated on April 6, 1926. The church is brick Romanesque with a slate roof. It is ironic that St. Aloysius Gonzaga was built by Germans to later become a part of the Italian "Hill" community.

SAINT ALPHONSUS LIGUORI "ROCK CHURCH"

Catholic
1868-72
1118 North Grand Blvd.
St. Louis, MO 63106
City Landmark: November 1974

On the invitation of Archbishop Kenrick the Redemptionist Fathers came to St. Louis in 1866. The Archbishop entrusted them with the administration of the Cathedral Parish until they could find a suitable location for their own church and monastery. Among these first Fathers were the Reverend Louis Dold, Superior; Egidins Smulders and Ferreol Girardey. Ground was broken on May 1, 1867 for the new church. The cornerstone was laid on November 3, 1867 by Very Reverend Joseph Melcher, Vicar-General of the archdiocese. The new church was dedicated on August 4, 1872. On July 10, 1872, the St. Louis house of the Redemptionist Fathers was raised to the dignity of a rectorate with Reverend W.V. Meredith as first rector. The growth of St. Alphonsus was quick with membership reaching about 800 families by 1910. The church maintains near that level today.

The church is stone in Gothic style and was designed by Reverend Louis Dold. The foundation was dug by the Redemptionist Brothers. The bells of the church weigh five tons and each one has its own name starting with the great St. Alphonsus bell and going down the scale of weight and up the scale of tone to the St. Joseph's bell, the St. Mary's bell and the St. Gabriel's bell. The altar, by Peter Theis of New York, is thirty-two feet high and eighteen feet wide and made of white carrara marble with panels of Mexican and Indian onyx. The church was known for its Novena's during 1931 which numbered its daily attendance at 18,460 average. The Tuesday Novena and solemn December Novena have been part of Rock history. The church windows were commissioned to Meyer of Munich shortly before the 1904 World's Fair. The windows were displayed at the fair as Meyer of Munich exhibit. The church steeple was completed in 1894 and stands 237 feet from the street to the top of the cross. The steeple was built by Conradi & Schrader of St. Louis. The cross is 19 feet high and weighs 1,500 pounds. St Alphonsus has been a parish church since 1881.

SAINT AMBROSE

Catholic
1926
5130 Wilson
St. Louis, MO 63110
National Historic Register

Originally, the large number of Italian Catholics residing in the southwestern part of St. Louis attended St. Aloysius Church where Reverend F.G. Holweck preached to them in their mother tongue. In 1903, they built their own frame church which they dedicated to St. Ambrose. The present structure was completed and dedicated in 1923. The Lombard Romanesque and brick structure was designed by Angelo Corrubia. The church was built entirely by Italian immigrants and is still considered an Italian church. The design of St. Ambrose is similar to the ancient San Ambrogio church in Milan where the body of St. Ambrose still lies on view in a specially built Basilica. St. Ambrose was the influential advisor of Emperor Theodosia in the fourth century. St. Ambrose now serves about 1200 families. The bronze statue near the entrance of the church is by Rudolph Torrini and is named "The Italian Immigrants."

SAINT ANDREW'S

Catholic
1930
309 Hoffmeister
St. Louis, MO 63125

In the spring of 1905, Reverend A. Mayer of Linn, Missouri received a call from the Archbishop to organize a new parish just south of the St. Louis city limits. Property was secured on Hoffmeister Road and erection of a temporary church was started on July 4, 1905. The two story frame building was blessed by Archbishop Glennon on December 17 of that year. This was a "mixed" parish, having both German and English speaking members. The present church, designed of brick in Italian Basilica style was built in 1930. The first service was Thanksgiving day, 1930. The church had 1400 families by 1946. St. Andrew's now serves about 2000 members in the LeMay, south county area.

SAINT ANDREW'S LUTHERAN

Lutheran (Mo Synod)
1932
6746 Etzel
University City, MO 63130

St. Andrew's Lutheran Church was organized in 1921 as an offshoot of the Lutheran Church in Wellston. The congregation first met in a frame building at Etzel and Sutter before moving to their present church at 6746 Etzel in 1932.

SAINT ANTHONY OF PADUA

Catholic
1908-10
3140 Meramec
St. Louis, MO 63118

St. Anthony's Parish was organized during the Civil War. During Christmas week, 1862, the Franciscan Father Servatius Almicks came to St. Louis and received Episcopal permission to found a Franciscan Convent in South St. Louis and also a parish which would be in the charge of the Fathers of that order. A tract of land at Compton and Meramec was purchased and erection of a small convent commenced. The cornerstone of the church, commonly called the "Monk's Church" was laid by Archbishop Kenrick. The church was consecrated in honor of St. Antonius of Padua, by Bishop Hogan of Kansas City on October

12, 1869. For 20 years, St. Anthony's was a mixed parish with both German and English speaking members. In 1882 the English speaking parishioners organized St. Thomas of Aquin nearby. After 1900, a new church was decided upon and it was built between 1908-1910. The church was designed by a Franciscan Brother, Anselm Wolf. The structure is brick of German Rhineland Romanesque design. The church is 226 feet long and the towers are 175 feet high. The original cost was $175,000. Stained glass is by Emil Frei of St. Louis and is considered a major piece of work by that company. The roof and interior of the church were extensively damaged by a fire in 1994, but it has since been restored. St. Anthony's serves about 1,100 members.

SAINT AUGUSTINE

Catholic
1896-1906 (Formerly St. Barbara's Catholic)
1371 Hamilton
St. Louis, MO 63112

In the 1880's, the Jesuit Fathers of Florissant built a chapel on a hill in west St. Louis in honor of St. Rose of Lima. The congregation later built a church at Goodfellow and Ethel avenues, leaving the old chapel vacant. In 1893, Reverend John Schramm was charged with building a new German parish in that part of the city, he purchased the property and used it as a temporary church for his St. Barbara congregation. On June 18, 1893, the first services were held in the now renovated chapel. By 1894, the parish had grown and a new church became a necessity. The cornerstone for this church was laid on May 6, 1896 by Archbishop Glennon and was dedicated by him on July 4, 1907. The church is of Gothic/Basilica design with transept of red brick. When the old St. Augustine church was closed, the congregation moved to the St. Barbara's church and the name was changed to St. Augustine

SAINT BONIFACE

Catholic
1860
7622 Michigan Avenue
St. Louis, MO 63111
Carondelet Historical Society

The cornerstone for St. Boniface Church was laid on the third Monday in May, 1860, by Vicar-General Joseph Melcher. Archbishop Kenrick dedicated the new church on December 26, 1860 in honor of the apostle of Germany, St. Boniface. The church was so poor that the contractor closed the doors for debt. The pastor, Father John Gamber had to ask the Archbishop for an advance to pay the bills. The second pastor, Reverend E.A. Schindel took charge in 1861 and by 1871, he not only paid the debt, but built a hospital south of the city. The structure is Italian Renaissance with Baroque detail and is made of brick and stone. It was designed by Thomas Brady of St. Louis. The south 100 foot tower was completed in 1868, the north one in 1890. New tower cupolas were added in 1969.

SAINT BRIDGET OF ERIN

Catholic
1860
2401 Carr Street
St. Louis, MO 63106

St. Bridget's Parish was founded in 1853 and was one of the most flourishing and prosperous parishes in St. Louis. St. Bridget's was considered the mother church of central St. Louis by 1910. The present church at Jefferson and Carr was erected in 1860 under the rectorship of Father William Walsh. At that time, it was the largest church in the city. In 1896, Pope Leo XIII appointed Father Walsh as a Domestic Prelate with the title of Monsignor, together with Msgr. H. Muehlsiepen and Msgr. Joseph Hessoun. Msgr. Walsh died in 1898 and was succeeded by Reverend Edward Fenlon and in 1907, by Reverend Patrick Dooley, who was formerly pastor of Assumption Parish in south St. Louis.

SAINT CECILIA

Catholic
1926
5418 Louisiana
St. Louis, MO 63111

In the spring of 1906, Reverend B.J. Benten, rector at St. Paul in St. Charles County, was charged with the organization of a new parish in south St. Louis. The site, at Eichelberger and Louisiana was purchased and a two-story brick building was erected based on plans by Wessbecher and Hillebrand. This building was replaced by the new one built in 1925-26. The cornerstone for the new St. Cecilia church was laid by Archbishop John J. Glennon on May 21, 1926. The church's pastor was Reverend B.J. Benten. The structure was designed by architect H.R. Hess. Stained glass is by Emil Frei of St. Louis

180

SAINT CHARLES BORROMEO

Catholic
1867 (Formerly St. John's Methodist Church)
2901 Locust Street
St. Louis, MO 63103

After the abandonment of St. Bonaventura church at Sixth and Spruce, the Italian Catholics in St. Louis worshipped at other churches in the city. Italian sermons were preached occasionally at St. Patrick's, St. Joseph's and St. Aloysius. In 1900, Reverend Caesar Spigardi came from New York to St. Louis and organized 10,000 Italian Catholics and rented the old Presbyterian church at Nineteenth and Morgan where they worshipped for two years. In 1902, the St. John's Methodist church at Twenty-ninth and Locust was purchased for $25,000 and one of the most flourishing parishes in the city was founded. The church had been built for St. John's in 1867. The church has been closed and abandoned for some time. The church is Gothic in style and was renovated by the Franciscans in 1957. The stained glass is by Emil Frei Art Glass of St. Louis.

SAINT CHARLES BORROMEO

Catholic
1916
601 North 4th Street
St. Charles, MO 63301

The first church of St. Charles Borromeo was made of log and was dedicated on November 7, 1791, the only church in the village that had previously been known as Les Petites Cotes (The Little Hills). The name of the village, settled by French-Canadian Louis Blanchette, was changed to St. Charles at that time in honor of the patron saint of the Spanish ruler, King Carlos III. The first pastor of the church was Father Bernard de Limpach.

The second church, of white stone, was built around 1827. It was outgrown by 1869 and a larger, red brick structure was erected on the site of the present church. That church was destroyed by a tornado in 1915. The cornerstone of the present church was laid in 1916, and the church of gray stone in Romanesque style was soon completed. The stained glass is by Emil Frei of St. Louis. The old church was the site of many marriages, baptisms and burials because it was the only church in St. Charles for many years and performed those services even for non-Catholics. Daniel Boone's son, David Morgan Boone married Sara Griffin there. The church cemetery holds the remains of such famous people as Jean Baptiste du Sable, the first settler of Chicago and St. Philippine Duchesne, who founded the Academy of the Sacred Heart and many other schools in the St. Louis area. A portrait of St. Charles Borromeo now hangs in the church. St. Charles Borromeo was the archbishop of Milan and a nephew of Pope Pius IV. Another church, now abandoned, at 2901 Locust in Downtown St. Louis also carries his name.

SAINT CRONAN

Catholic
1879
1203 South Boyle
St. Louis, MO 63110

St. Cronan's Parish was founded out of part of the territory of St. James Parish in 1879 by Reverend Thomas A. Butler. services were held in a hall until a church was built. On April 9, 1879, the cornerstone for a small brick church, part of the present church was laid at Boyle and Swan avenues. The church was dedicated on July 27, 1879. The congregation developed rapidly and two additions were made in a short time.

SAINT CYRIL & METHODIUS

Polish National Catholic
1857 (Formerly North Presbyterian)
North 11th & Chambers
St. Louis, MO 63106
National Historic Register: June 28, 1982

This church was designed in 1857 by Eugene L. Greenleaf of St. Louis and represents one of the few surviving examples of Lombard Romanesque Revival style. The building, used originally by the North Presbyterian church, is one of the oldest churches in St. Louis. In 1908, St. Cyril and Methodius Church was organized as part of the Polish National Catholic Churches. This faction is the largest American schism of Roman Catholicism and originated in Scranton, Pennsylvania in 1896. The church abolished compulsory celibacy for clergy in 1921. St. Cyril & Methodius is the first Polish National Church west of the Mississippi and one of the oldest in the country today. The church is part of the National Historic district that is named for the church.

SAINT ENGELBERT

Catholic
1891
4330 Shreve Avenue
St. Louis, MO 63115

St. Engelbert's Parish was organized Easter Sunday, March 30, 1891 when the area was mostly occupied by truck gardens and dairymen. The first meeting was at the home of Mr. Engelbert Schaper on Bircher Street. Reverend Anton Pauk was the first rector. The cornerstone for the first church at Marcus and Carter was laid May 31, 1891, by Vicar-General H. Muehlsiepen. The building, costing $23,000 was dedicated in honor of St. Engelbert on Sunday, November 22, 1891 by the Vicar-General. The church had a frontage of fifty feet and a depth of eighty feet. The second story was used for the church with the first story used as a school and sister's dwelling. The parish, which is west of Calvary Cemetery, grew quickly and was recognized very early as being one of the most promising in North St. Louis. The congregation soon outgrew the first church and this new one was constructed.

SAINT FERDINAND

Catholic
1821
1 Rue St. Francois
Florissant, MO 63031
National Historic Register:

St. Ferdinand is one of the oldest parishes in the Mississippi Valley, dating its origin from the first settlement of the Jesuits in Florissant Valley in 1792. Florissant or San Fernando as it was known then, was part of the territory described in 1798 as being among "The settlements of his Catholic Majesty in Ylinda" by Zenon Trudeau, the Spanish Lieutenant-Governor of Upper Louisiana. Although a Spanish settlement, Florissant had many residents of French stock, many of them from Canada. French was the recognized language and its Catholic heritage is reflected in the street names following those of the Saints. The first church, built near St. Ferdinand, St. Louis and St. Charles streets was built in 1789. The first pastor of this church was probably the Capuchin Friar, Bernard de Limpach. He had been the second resident pastor of St. Louis and remained in charge of St. Ferdinand until he died in 1796. This first log church was destroyed by fire in 1836.

On February 19, 1821, St. Ferdinand's pastor, Father De La Croix laid the cornerstone of the new church, the stone being a gift from Mother Philippine Duchesne, to whom he had previously rendered services. It was the choice of Mother Duchesne that St. Regis, along with St. Ferdinand would be one of the patron Saints of the new church. The church was blessed and dedicated on November 21, 1821, by Father De La Croix, assisted by Father Acquaroni, pastor of Portage Des Sioux. The church was finally consecrated by Bishop Rosati, September 2, 1832. The church is built of red brick in Wings Federal design.

In February, 1831, Father Theodore De Theux, previously the pastor of St. Ferdinand, became superior of the Missouri Jesuit Mission. In August of that year, he fixed his headquarters at Florissant and opened a Noviate which was named St. Stanlislaus Seminary.

Father Peter J. De Smet, S.J., known as the apostle of the Indians, was ordained at St. Ferdinand September 23, 1827. He died in 1873 and is buried at St. Stanlislaus. The first motherhouse in the United States of the Society of the Sacred Heart was established by St. Rose Philippine Duchesne shortly after her arrival in St. Louis in 1818. Mother Duchesne was canonized by the Catholic Church July 3, 1988. Archbishop Joseph Ritter closed St. Ferdinand in 1955. Until 1958, the parish was overseen by Priests of the Jesuit Society and the school was staffed by The Sisters of Loretto. St. Ferdinand is believed to be the oldest brick Catholic church west of the Mississippi River and east of the Rockies. The old church is now maintained as a Shrine by The Friends of Old St. Ferdinand and the new St. Ferdinand church serves the parish of 2000 families on Charbonier Road.

SAINT FRANCIS XAVIER

Catholic
1897
3628 Lindell Blvd.
St. Louis, MO 63108
City Landmark: November 1974

The history of St. Francis Xavier (College Church) is closely interwoven with that of St. Louis University. When the Jesuit Fathers erected their university at Ninth and Washington avenues in 1928, they also built a chapel dedicated in honor of St. Aloysius, which served as a house of worship for the few scattering Catholics in the sparsely settled vicinity. Since this chapel formed the nucleus for a congregation, it is only proper to date the organization of the parish from that year. In 1841, a new church was built on Ninth and Christy Avenue and dedicated in honor of St. Francis Xavier. The St. Aloysius chapel was then turned over to the German Catholics of North St. Louis until they were able to build a church of their own. The St. Francis Xavier Parish flourished here for sixty years. In 1884, when St. Louis University was moved to its present location on Grand Avenue, the building of a new church was commenced and the cornerstone laid in the summer of 1884. The basement of the church was opened for divine worship on All Saint's Day (November 1), 1884. Reverend Michael Corbett, S.J. was then pastor. The church was dedicated in 1898 after being mostly completed. The 201 foot spire was not completed until 1915. The church is 211 1/2 feet in length.

The church is an example of 19th century Revival English Gothic of the transition period and was designed by Irish-born Architect Thomas Waryng Walsh. He died before it was finished and the design was somewhat modified by Henry Switzer of Chicago. The structure is of North St. Louis Limestone, ornamented with Bedford stone from Indiana. Both inside and out, it closely resembles St. Colman's Cathedral in Cobb. Ireland. The exterior of St. Francis Xavier was completely cleaned and restored in 1984 and the interior renovated in 1989-90. The bells, moved from the old church at Ninth and Christy, were cast in Spain in the 18th century. The stained glass windows are by Emil Frei of St. Louis. St. Louis University lays claim to being the oldest college west of the Mississippi.

SAINT FRANCIS DE SALES

Catholic
1907
2653 Ohio
St. Louis, MO 63118
National Historic Register: November 2, 1978
City Landmark: April, 1971

The rapid growth of St. Peter and Paul's Parish necessitated the establishment of another German parish just to the west. The first step was made April 22, 1867, when twenty-nine gentlemen met and decided to purchase a lot on Ohio and Lynch in the so-called "Dangerfield Tract." The building of the church was commenced immediately and on Christmas Day, 1867 services were held in the new church. The first church was soon outgrown by the congregation and the cornerstone for the new one was laid August 11,

1895 by Vicar-General Henry Muehlsiepen. The tornado of May 27, 1896 destroyed the old church, saving the congregation the trouble of dismantling it. The congregation had to meet in the school hall and then in the new basement until the church was finally completed on May 27, 1908. The $275,000 structure was dedicated by Bishop John Janssen of Belleville, Illinois on Thanksgiving Day, (November 27), 1909. Bishop Meerschaerdt of Oklahoma, preached the English and Abbot Ignatius Conrad, of New Subiaco, Arkansas, the German sermon.

The original plans for the church were drawn by Engelbert Seibertz of Berlin, modified by Victor J. Klutho of Klutho & Ranft of St. Louis in 1906. The design is German Gothic Revival with the 300 foot steeple being the tallest in the city. The interior of the church was frescoed in 1916 by Fridolin Fuchs in Basilica style. The stained glass is by Emil Frei of St. Louis.

SAINT GEORGE

Catholic
1915
8300 Gravois
St. Louis, MO 63123

SAINT HEDWIG

Catholic
1904
3202 Pulaski
St. Louis, MO 63111

In 1904, Reverend Victor Stepka was charged by the Archbishop to organize a new Polish parish in south St. Louis. A church and school building, dedicated to St. Hedwig, was erected on Compton Avenue and Hiawatha Street. The parish numbered 150 families by 1910. In 1906, Reverend Stepka was succeeded by Reverend S.J. Zielinski. The church address is now on Pulaski Street due to the street name changes.

SAINT JACOBI

Evangelical Lutheran
1906-22
8646 Jennings Road
St. Louis, MO 63136

194

SAINT JAMES COMMUNITY CENTER
1867 (Formerly St. Jacob Deutsche Evangelical)
1455 East College
St. Louis, MO 63107

SAINT JAMES MISSIONARY BAPTIST

Missionary Baptist
1913 (Formerly Hope Congregational)
1644 Semple
St. Louis, MO 63112

The Hope Congregational Church was designed by architect G. Howard and built of brick at a cost of $18,000. The permit was taken out August 6, 1913 and the cornerstone laid that same year. Like many north city churches, this one has had the original cornerstone information removed or covered.

SAINT JAMES THE GREATER

Catholic
1928
6401 Wade
St. Louis, MO 63139

Several years before the territory which now forms St. James Parish became part of St. Louis, a Catholic parish was organized near Cheltenham by Reverend P. Kelly. The congregation was formed originally in 1860 as a mission of St. Malachy. The young parish showed evidence of solid growth and a modest church was erected at 1368 Tamm Avenue and dedicated in honor of St. James in 1861. The present church at Tamm and Wade was built and competed in August, 1928 was dedicated October 7, 1928. The church, designed by O'Meara and Hills, is 11th century English Gothic style. St. James the Greater is the focal point of the Dogtown neighborhood, an Irish-Italian enclave immediately south of Forest Park. St. James the Greater has always been and continues to be a vital presence in the community. The parish serves about 750 families.

SAINT JOHN & SAINT JAMES

Catholic
1925
140 North Elizabeth Avenue
Ferguson, MO 63135

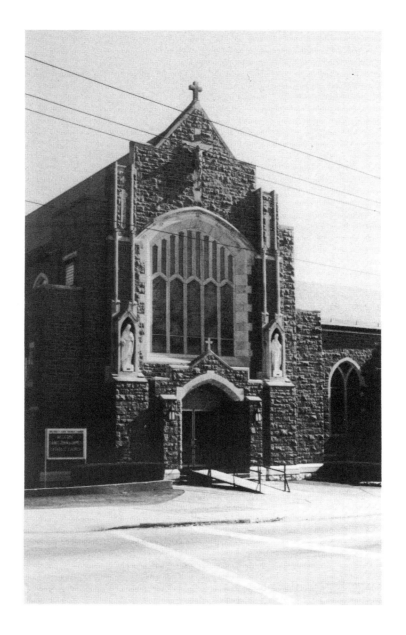

SAINT JOHN A.M.E.
African Methodist Episcopal
1925 (Formerly Salem Methodist)
1908 North Kingshighway
St. Louis, MO 63113

This church, built in 1925, was the fourth location of the Salem Methodist Church. The Salem congregation moved to this location from the previous church on Page. The St. John A.M.E. purchased the building in 1957 and removed the original identifying cornerstone. Salem Methodist moved to its present location at Lindbergh and Highway 40 in West St. Louis County.

SAINT JOHN NEPOMUK

Catholic
1870-72
1625 South 11th
St. Louis, MO 63104
National Historic Register: June 19, 1972
City Landmark: April, 1971

The Bohemian Catholics of south city were organized in 1854 by Right Reverend Francis de Sales Goller of St. Peter & Paul Parish. With Reverend Henry Lipovsky as the first pastor, a frame church was built at 11th and Lafayette and dedicated in 1855. The first High Mass was sung by the famous Indian missionary Father Peter J. DeSmet. Through the efforts of Reverend Joseph Hessoun, who assumed control of the parish in 1855, St. John Nepomuk became not only a very prosperous parish, but the center of the Bohemian-America Catholics of the United States. This church is the oldest Bohemian Catholic church in America. Father Hessoun was called the "'Apostle of the Bohemians in America."

As the congregation outgrew their original church, a new, brick structure was built in 1870-72 at a cost of $50,000. The tornado of May 27, 1896 destroyed this church, but it was rebuilt by late 1897 from plans by Adolphus Druiding. The windows in the new church are from 1929 and were from Emil Frei Art Glass in St. Louis. The church contains many wooden statues from Bohemia which were spared by the tornado. On July 4, 1909, the Bohemian Catholics of St. Louis dedicated their new orphanage at Fenton, in St. Louis County. The Institute was called the Hessoun Orphanage in memory of the late Monsignor Hessoun, who died July 4, 1906.   The Bohemian or Czech community around St. John Nepomuk became what was called "Bohemian Hill" and grew to 5000 residents. They also built St. Wenceslaus Catholic church on Oregon.

SAINT JOHN THE APOSTLE & EVANGELIST

Catholic
1860
15 Plaza Square
St. Louis, MO 63103
City Landmark: March, 1971

The westward growth of St. Louis necessitated the organization of a new parish west of the mother-church St. Patrick's. In November, 1847, Father Patrick O'Brien was charged with the founding of the new congregation which was named in honor of St. John, the Apostle and Evangelist. This was the eighth Catholic parish in St. Louis. A small brick church was built and dedicated the following spring by Archbishop Kenrick. it was not long before a larger church became necessary. The cornerstone for the new church was laid February 2, 1859 and the church was dedicated the first Sunday in November, 1860. The structure is Lombard Renaissance Revival style of red brick. The design work was started by Thomas Walsh, but he resigned in a controversy over the viability of the plans. The plans were completed by Patrick Walsh. The church is 66 1/2 feet by 113 feet with twin 100 foot towers. In 1876, St. John's Church became the Pro-Cathedral of St. Louis by Archbishop Kenrick as the old Cathedral was becoming more and more surrounded by business and industrial establishments. When Archbishop J. J. Kain was called to the Archiepiscopal See of St. Louis, he re-established his Cathedral in the Old Cathedral, residing at the archbishop's residence at 3810 Lindell Blvd. By the end of the 19th century, St. John's met the fate of all of the other downtown parishes and became known as the parish of the poor. St. John's was remodeled in 1961 by Murphy & Mackey of St. Louis and is one of the two downtown churches spared during demolitions for the Plaza Square Apartments.

SAINT JOHN THE BAPTIST

Catholic
1930
4200 Delor
St. Louis, MO 63116

The Cornerstone for St. John the Baptist was laid by Archbishop John J. Glennon on June 1, 1930.

SAINT JOHN'S EPISCOPAL

Episcopal
1907
3664 Arsenal
St. Louis, MO 63116

St. John's Episcopal Church was founded October 12, 1841 at Christ Church at Fifth and Chestnut with official organization effected December 28, 1841. First services were held in the Washington Engine House on Second Street near Plum. In 1842, it was decided to erect a brick church at Fifth and Spruce. In 1852, a lot was purchased at Sixth and Spruce streets and a cornerstone laid September 2, 1852. By 1868, the church had decided to move and a lot was purchased at Hickory and Dolman streets. The new church was completed in 1871. There were structural problems and the new church was not consecrated until December 27, 1889. The cornerstone for the present church was laid December 1, 1907. First services were held on September 20, 1908. The 1200 pound octagonal pulpit designed and built in London is on permanent loan from St. Peter's Episcopal in Ladue. The pulpit dates from 1896.

SAINT JOHN'S EVANGELICAL
United Church of Christ
1922 (Formerly St. John's Evangelical)
11333 St. John's Church Road
St. Louis, MO 63123

In 1838, under the leadership of Reverend Edward Louis Nollau and 15 of the German settlers of the area known as Gravois Settlement, St. John's Evangelical Church was formed. The first church building was built in 1839. St. John's was one of the first Evangelical churches west of the Mississippi. In 1840, the Evangelical Synod of North America was formed at St. John's Church. By 1868, St. John's had grown so much that a new church was needed. A fine brick structure was erected and dedicated. By 1922, the present brick Gothic church, designed by architect A. Meyers was built. The first service and dedication was Christmas Eve, 1922. The Evangelical Church later became the Evangelical & Reformed. In 1957, the Evangelical & Reformed Church became part of the newly formed United Church of Christ.

SAINT JOHN'S UNITED CHURCH OF CHRIST

United Church of Christ
1922 (Formerly St. John's Evangelical)
4138 North Grand
St. Louis, MO 63107

SAINT JOHN'S UNITED CHURCH OF CHRIST
United Church of Christ
1869
531 Jackson
St. Charles, MO 63301

SAINT JOHN'S UNITED METHODIST

United Methodist
1901-03
5000 Washington Ave.
St. Louis, MO 63108
City Landmark: January, 1972

On July 2, 1864, a decision was reached at a quarterly conference at Asbury Church to build a new Methodist church in St. Louis. Six months later the ground for the new church was purchased at 29th and Locust, and on July 27, 1867, the cornerstone was laid. The official date for the organization of the congregation was October 18, 1868 when the chapel was finished and dedicated. The church was completed the following spring and given the name St. John's Methodist Episcopal, South. The new church was dedicated on May 9, 1869. In 1900 it was felt that the church should move as far west as Kingshighway to keep up with the growing city. In 1901 ground was broken for the new church at Kingshighway and Washington. The new church was dedicated October 5, 1902 with Bishop W.A. Candier preaching. The church is limestone Classical revival from plans by Theodore C. Link. The structure has Ionic Porticoes. New interiors from 1945 include windows by Siegfried Reinhardt of St. Louis when he was an artist for Emil Frei Art Glass. Other windows from 1967 are by Rodney Winfield of St. Louis

In 1927 the new chapel and education building designed by Wilbur Trueblood were begun and completed in August of 1928. St. John's was directly responsible for the establishment of the Methodist Home for children, Kingdom House, Barnes Hospital and Gambrill Gardens Retirement Homes. Two of St. John's ministers, John Moore and Ivan Lee Holt, have become bishops. St. John's is part of the Holy Corners Historical District.

SAINT JOSEPH'S

Catholic
1912
106 North Meramec
Clayton, MO 63105

This church then known as St. Martin's was formerly located at Central Post Office at the intersection of Price and Bonhomme roads. The site of Centerton Park identifies the location of the old church today. When the old church was torn down, the bricks were used for the new rectory at Clayton. The church was moved to Clayton and a frame structure built in 1869 by Reverend J.B. Jackson. By 1910, the parish numbered about 200 families and was growing rapidly. The parish at that time consisted mostly of Irish-Americans with a heavy sprinkling of German-Americans and a few French families. The present brick church was built in 1912.

SAINT JOSEPH CROATION

Catholic
1928
2112 South 12th
St. Louis, MO 63104
City Landmark

In 1904 the Croatian Catholics of St. Louis were organized into a parish by Reverend Oskar Suster. They purchased the Jewish synagogue at Thirteenth Street and Chouteau Avenue and fitted it up as a very neat Catholic church. They began holding services there in 1906. The congregation later moved and built a new church in south city. The present structure at 2112 South Twelfth Street was built on the former Ursuline Convent property and is of brick and stone in Romanesque design. The new church was dedicated by Archbishop Glennon on April 26, 1928. St. Joseph is the only Croatian Roman Catholic Church in the state of Missouri.

SAINT JOSEPH'S SHRINE

Catholic
1846-1880
1220 North 11th Street
St. Louis, MO 63106
National Historic Register: May 19, 1978
City Landmark: August, 1973

The Jesuit Fathers of St. Louis had given to the German-American Catholics of North St. Louis the use of St. Aloysius Chapel on Tenth Street and Washington Avenue and attended to them until 1844, when the organization of a new German parish was decided upon. With the approval of Archbishop Kenrick, the Jesuits undertook the work of organization. Mrs. Ann Biddle donated a lot for the purpose on Eleventh and Biddle streets. The cornerstone for the church was laid April 21, 1846 and the church dedicated on the first Sunday in August 1846 in honor of St. Joseph by Reverend Van de Velde, Provincial of the Jesuits. The cost of the church was $10,776. The first pastor, Reverend P. Patchowski was succeeded in 1847 by Reverend Father Seisl, S.J. It was through his efforts that the German St. Vincent's Orphan Society and first orphanage was created on Hogan Street. On July 21, 1863, the men of the parish met and decided to enlarge the church and build a rectory. In the Autumn of 1865, the cornerstone was laid by Archbishop Kenrick and the new addition dedicated on December 30, 1866.

The growth at that period came in part from the first miracle in 1864. A German immigrant was cured after kissing the relic of Blessed Peter Clavier. This was one of three miracles submitted to the Vatican which resulted in the canonization of this Jesuit missionary in 1888. Another miracle was the saving of parishioners from the cholera plague in 1866 after making a solemn pledge to St. Joseph, that if spared, they would have a beautiful altar later built which today is known as "The Altar of Answered Prayers." By 1870, St. Joseph's was the largest parish in the city, numbering 1000 families. In 1880, the congregation decided to tear down the front of the church and rebuilt it in accordance with the style of the new addition. This new front was completed in 1881. This addition included the Baroque facade and flanking towers that are part of the church today. This addition was designed by Adolphus Druiding of St. Louis. The large upper cupolas of the towers were removed in 1954. By 1944, only 20 families remained in St. Joseph's Parish. Control was passed to the Archdiocese in 1965. Rumors that St. Joseph's would be razed led to the Landmark's Association's decision in 1976 to hold their membership meeting there and to engage architect Ted Wofford to study renovation costs. That report led to the organization of the Friends of St. Joseph, which today sees to the preservation efforts of the Shrine.

SAINT LAWRENCE O'TOOLE

Catholic
1864
1237 14th Street
St. Louis, MO 63106

In the year 1855, when St. Lawrence O'Toole's parish was organized, St. Louis had about 25,000 residents. The western city limits were about Seventeenth Street. Where St. Lawrence O'Toole is located was then an unbroken succession of ponds and prairies traversed here and there by primitive corduroy roads. In 1855 Archbishop P.R. Kenrick gave James Henry, then a newly ordained priest, the mission of organizing a new parish west of the mother-church. On April 19, 1855, Archbishop Kenrick laid the cornerstone for a temporary church. It was a modest brick structure dedicated to the Feast of St. Lawrence O'Toole, November 14 of that same year. In 1862, building of the new church was commenced. This building was completed in the fall of 1864 and was dedicated on the Feast of St. Gertrude before a most distinguished assemblage of dignitaries and laity. The church was almost destroyed by a tornado in 1865, but was finally completed.

It was of Gothic design, without transept, 75 by 150 feet of brick and stone. Father Henry's indefatigable zeal and energy soon placed the parish in the front ranks of St. Louis parishes, He died at Liverpool, England on November 5, 1891. His remains were brought back to St. Louis and interred at Calvary Cemetery. By 1910, the parish numbered about 300 families. The interior of this church was frescoed. There were four altars of marble with a main altar that held three marble medallions supposedly carved by the sculptor who accompanied Emperor Maximilian to Mexico. A portion of the walls of the first level is all that remains today of the old church, which now serves as a truck repair garage.

SAINT LIBORIUS

Catholic
1889
1835 North 18th Street
St. Louis, MO 63106
National Historic Register: October 11, 1979
City Landmark: April, 1975

St. Liborius was the sixth German parish in St. Louis. On October 30, 1855 a lot was purchased on North Market and Hogan streets and the cornerstone of the new church was laid by Vicar-General Melcher on June 15, 1856. The building was dedicated on January 25, 1857 and consecrated by Archbishop Kenrick on July 17, 1859. Growth soon made a larger church necessary and the cornerstone was laid on June 10, 1888, by Vicar-General Henry Muehlsiepen. On November 24, 1889, the new church was dedicated. The Gothic Revival, red brick structure was designed by William Schickel of New York. The high altar was done by contractors Bothe & Ratermann, parishoners. Emil Frei installed new windows in 1907. St. Liborius was known as "The Cathedral of the North Side." The parish is now closed.

SAINT LOUIS CATHEDRAL

Catholic
1914
4431 Lindell Blvd.
St. Louis, MO 63108
City Landmark: September, 1973

On October 28, 1896, Archbishop John Joseph Kain issued a pastoral letter announcing the selection and purchase of the block bounded by Taylor, Newstead, Maryland and Lindell. This action laid the groundwork for what would come to be known as The New Cathedral. Although Archbishop Kain died in October of 1903, his dream did not end. On May 1, 1907, Archbishop John J. Glennon broke the first ground for the structure. The cornerstone was laid by Archbishop Glennon on October 18, 1908. After a special competition directed by a committee selected by the Archbishop, architectural design was accomplished by St. Louis architect George D. Barnett of the firm of Barnett, Haynes & Barnett who had also designed the Shrine of the Sacred Heart in 1898. The new church was created in Romanesque exterior/Byzantine interior style in gray granite and measures 204 X 350 feet with a 217 foot high central dome. The twin towers are 157 feet high.

Although the completed structure was blessed and the first Mass was celebrated on October 18, 1914, Archbishop Glennon pledged that the cathedral would not be finished until "it has set on its walls the luster of every jewel, the bright plumage of every bird, the glow and glory of every metal, the iridescent gleam of every glass." It took more than fifty-six years for that task to be completed, and it took some of the finest artists and artisans in the world. The two chapels on the west corner were designed by Aristide Leonori and done by Tiffany and Company of New York in 1912. Tiffany also created the large rose window. The high altar, designed by George D. Barnett was erected in 1913 by Gorham Company of New York. August Wagner, Inc. of Berlin sent Paul Heuduck to St. Louis in 1923 to decorate the cathedral with mosaics. He joined with Emil Frei Art Glass of St. Louis to form the Ravenna Mosaic Company. Work on the mosaics continued into the 1960's. These mosaics are now refuted to be the most valuable collection in the world. The mosaics are of stone and glass. A layer of pure gold leaf is placed on glass and covered with a thin glass film. The pressed glass is then cut into small cubes, or tesserae about one half inch square; these pieces are used with colored stones to produce a picture. The colored stones are cut in irregular shapes and placed at various angles to give infinite variability to the effects achieved by tones and light. It is estimated that more than one hundred million pieces of stone and glass were used in this 84,000 square foot expanse of art. St. Louis Cathedral is recognized to be the foremost example of a Byzantine style church in the Americas. The solemn consecration of the edifice took place on June 29, 1926, His Eminence, John Cardinal Bonzano presiding.

SAINT LOUIS PARK BAPTIST

Baptist
1889 (Formerly First German Baptist)
2629 Rauschenbach
St. Louis, MO 63106

SAINT LUCAS

United Church of Christ
1905
11735 Denny Road
St. Louis, MO 63126

St. Lucas German Evangelical Church was formed in 1880. The German language was still being used as late as 1925. The congregation originally met in a frame structure on the present site. The cemetery behind the church holds the graves of church members whose births date back to the early 1800's. This structure, built of stone was built in 1905. The Evangelical Church, later Evangelical & Reformed became part of the United Church of Christ when that group was formed in 1957. The facility has been updated in 1955, 1968, 71 and 83. Later stained glass work designed by Francis Deck was accomplished by Emil Frei of St. Louis. The church now serves about 1770 members.

SAINT LUKE & MEMORIAL BAPTIST

Baptist
1941
3619 Finney
St. Louis, MO 63113

St. Luke and Memorial Baptist Churches were consolidated September 15, 1940 with Reverend J. House as pastor. On September 21, 1941 the congregation moved into the present structure which was formerly the home of the Ancient Order of Hibernians.

SAINT MARCUS EVANGELICAL
United Church of Christ
1914 (St. Marcus Evangelical & Reformed)
2102A Russell
St. Louis, MO 63104

St. Marcus Evangelical & Reformed Church was founded in 1843 and held its first service in the old Benton School on Sixth Street near Locust. In 1848 a new church building was erected at Jackson and Soulard streets. St. Peters Church in North St. Louis was erected at the same time. The church later moved to Third and Lafayette Avenue. In 1914, St. Marcus moved to its present location at McNair and Russell avenues. St. Marcus Church has operated a cemetery almost from its inception. The first was located on Carroll Street in the 1840's. Later a tract of land was acquired at Gravois and Kingshighway and the present cemetery was opened there in 1856. The Evangelical & Reformed Church became part of the United Church of Christ in 1957.

SAINT MARGARET OF SCOTLAND

Catholic
1906
3854 Flad
St. Louis, MO 63110

When the needs of an English speaking parish north of Tower Grove Park became obvious, Archbishop Glennon charged Reverend J.J. O'Brien, then senior assistant at St. Leo's Church, with the formation of the new parish. A vacant store building on the south-east corner of Russell and Vandeventer avenues was rented and the store arranged as a temporary church. It soon became apparent that the new parish would be a success and planning began for a new church. A fine site was purchased at Flad and Vandeventer and the erection of a church building, designed by Barnett, Haynes and Barnett was undertaken. The cornerstone was laid by Vicar-General O.S.J. Hoog in 1906. The church was blessed by Archbishop Glennon on Thanksgiving Day, 1908 in honor of St. Margaret. Later stained glass work is by Emil Frei.

SAINT MARK'S COMMUNITY CENTER
1901 (Formerly St. Mark's Catholic)
1313 Academy
St. Louis, MO 63113

In April of 1893, Reverend John J. Dilon was commissioned to found a new parish in the north-western part of St. Louis. He bought a suitable site at Page and Academy and a temporary church was soon built. By 1899, St. Mark's Parish had developed and grown and the congregation, under pastor Reverend Peter J. O'Rourke proceeded to build a new church. The cornerstone was laid July 9, 1901, and the church blessed by Archbishop Glennon in November of 1902. The church was designed by Barnett, Haynes and Barnett. It is of pure Colonial Gothic, built of Bedford limestone and cost $82,000. The clergy of St. Mark's attended to the spiritual needs of Christian Brothers College which was in its immediate neighborhood at the time. The old church is now the home of St. Mark's Community Center.

SAINT MARK'S EPISCOPAL

Episcopal
1939
4714 Clifton Avenue
St. Louis, MO 63109
City Landmark: September, 1973

This white brick church, designed by architect Frederick Dunn of Dunn & Nagel is considered and outstanding example of the "Art Deco" or "Moderne" style and was one of the earliest churches in North America built in this architectural style. St. Mark's was the city's first contemporary church. The stained glass designed by Robert Harmon and crafted by Emil Frei, is also considered an outstanding example of its kind and has interesting 1930's social and political motifs. There is a fine Aeolian Skinner organ, Opus 797, 1939. The bell in the churchyard came from England and is dated 1636. The limestone statue of St. Mark on the front elevation is by Sheila Burlingame. St. Mark's congregation was a merger of Holy Innocent's and St. Andrew's.

SAINT MARK'S EVANGELICAL LUTHERAN
Evangelical Lutheran (ELCA)
1919-21
6337 Clayton Road
Clayton, MO 63105

St. Mark's was organized March 8, 1867 as the first and for many years the only Lutheran Church in St. Louis to use English language in its services. First services were held at Asbury Methodist Episcopal church at Fifteenth near Franklin and Morgan (now Delmar). The cornerstone for St. Mark's first home, on Elliot Avenue near Wash was laid September 6, 1868 with the dedication February 21, 1869. It was not finally completed until January 21, 1872. The first pastor was Reverend Dr. S.W. Harkey. The congregation grew and the city changed so that in November of 1880. property was purchased to erect a new church at Cardinal & Bell. The cornerstone was laid May 29, 1881. and the new church dedicated October 1, 1882. The congregation moved again and a new cornerstone was laid at 6999 Clayton Avenue (Now 6337 Clayton Rd.) on September 19, 1919. The church was dedicated April 21, 1921.

In later years, the English Lutheran Church became part of the group of ethnic Lutheran churches that combined to form the Lutheran Church in America. Throughout the years, St. Mark's has had nine of its members become ordained into the ministry.

SAINT MARY AND JOSEPH

Catholic
1940
6304 Minnesota
St. Louis, MO 63111

As early as 1775, a lot between Second and Third streets in Carondelet, then called Prairie Catalan, had been set aside for a church and cemetery. In 1823, the first church was erected by direction of Bishop DuBourg. It was a modest rough board hut and dedicated in honor of Our Lady of Mt. Carmel. The old church was replaced by a log structure built west of the first church in 1835. A new, large brick church, dedicated to St. Mary & Joseph, was built north of the old one in 1859 which served until the cornerstone for the present structure was laid by Archbishop Glennon September 22, 1940.

SAINT MARY MAGDALEN

Catholic
1944
2618 South Brentwood
St. Louis, MO 63144

SAINT MARY OF VICTORIES

Catholic
1843
744 South 3rd Street
St. Louis, MO 63102
National Historic Register: August 28, 1980
City Landmark: January, 1973

As early as 1834 special services were held for German-Catholics at the Old Cathedral, which at that time, was the only Catholic church in St. Louis. By 1842, the German-Catholic population had reached 7000 and the organization of a German parish became necessary. A lot on Third and Gratiot streets was donated by a Mrs. Hunt. The other half of the lot was donated by Mrs Hunt's brother, J.H. Lucas and the building of the new church began. The cornerstone was laid June 23, 1843 and dedicated September 15, 1844 in honor of St. Mary of Victories. The simple brick Classical Revival structure with monumental doorway was designed by George I. Barnett and Francis Saler of St. Louis. The church was enlarged in 1855 by addition of the transept and tower. Another story was added in 1868. Restoration accomplished in 1941

228

SAINT MARY'S

Catholic
1898
525 East 4th Street
Alton, IL 62002

SAINT MATTHEW

United Church of Christ
1889
2613 Potomac Street
St. Louis, MO 63118

St. Matthew's Evangelical & Reformed Church was organized on Reformation Sunday, October 31, 1875 in a room at 2622 South Broadway. Reverend Henry Braschler was the first pastor. There were 40 charter members. The cornerstone of the first church building, located at Seventh & Cave streets, was laid November 28, 1875 and dedicated March 5, 1876. The church purchased 45 acres at Bates and Morganford in 1878 for St. Matthew Cemetery. A chapel was built in 1887 and an additional 10 acres was added in 1892. The present red brick structure at Jefferson and Potomac was built in 1882 for $36,641.80. In 1957, St. Matthew became part of the United Church of Christ. During the 1930's and 1940's, St. Matthew had as many as 1000 members. The church serves about 110 families today.

SAINT MATTHEW THE APOSTLE

Catholic
1906-13
2715 North Sarah
St. Louis, MO 63113
National Historic Register: August 6, 1986

St. Matthews Parish was organized in 1893 by Reverend Joseph T. Shields. A temporary church and school served the parish of about 450 families until the new church was built. In 1906 the beautiful new church was erected from plans by Joseph Conradi of St. Louis. The structure is English Gothic Revival in stone with transept. The interior features star vaulting. The Tudor Gothic rectory was designed by McMahon in 1919. St. Matthews reached its peak during the World War I era with a congregation of about 1500 families. In the late 1950's, the parish led the city in the number of black conversions to Catholicism. The school was recycled to housing by Westminster Builders in 1986 from plans by James Bartl of St. Louis.

SAINT MICHAEL & SAINT GEORGE

Episcopal
1913
6345 Wydown
Clayton, MO 63105

St George's was organized in 1845 and its first church was located on the northwest corner of Locust and Seventh Street. The building, designed by George Barnett was dedicated by Bishop Hawks on 13 April, 1848. After the Civil War, St. George's moved to what was known as Stoddard's Addition at Beaumont and Chestnut. This new $125,000 church with its 145 foot tower was completed in the spring of 1874.

George had to turn to Christ Church Cathedral for help. The church was consolidated and became St. George's Chapel of Christ Church Cathedral. The parish was able to regain stability and became independent again in 1919.

Several miles west, the Church of St. Michael and All Angels was growing and thriving. This church was organized in 1912 as the brain child of bishop Daniel S. Tuttle. A church was to be built, based on a private donation of $50,000. A committee selected a triangular lot at the intersection of Wydown and Ellenwood in what was then known as Skinker Heights. This site was occupied by the Sunny Brook Distillery during the 1904 World's Fair. On Christmas Day, 1913, services were held for the first time in the newly completed English Gothic building. The church, rectory and parish house were designed by James P. Jamieson, the architect who designed the early buildings on the Washington University campus. The buildings are all of Missouri red granite trimmed with Bedford, Indiana limestone. In October, 1928, St. George's church merged with St. Michael and All Angels and the merged parish was given the name The Church of St. Michael and St. George. At about the same time, work was begun to enlarge the church to its present capacity of 660. The chancel was extended to the east and the original sanctuary was cut free and relocated. The altar in the church is from St. George's and the cross and candleholders are from the Church of St. Michael and All Angels. The total cost of the reconstruction was $350,000. Part of the stained glass work was designed by Robert Harmon and Francis Deck and accomplished by Emil Frei of St. Louis.

SAINT MICHAEL THE ARCHANGEL

Catholic
1948
7622 Sutherland
St. Louis, MO, 63119

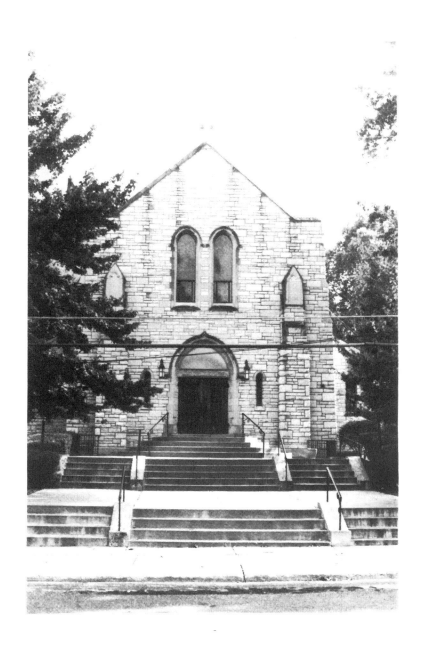

SAINT MICHAEL THE ARCHANGEL

Russian Orthodox
1929
1901 Ann Avenue
St. Louis, MO 63104

The St. Michael's Parish was made up of immigrants from parts of Europe such as Austria-Hungary, Galacia and Russia. Before its formal organization in October, 1909, the congregation originally met jointly with the Greek Orthodox congregation. The group then met in rented store buildings until 1910 when it purchased a house at 1125 Hickory Street for $7,000. This was used until the present structure was completed. The parish began planning for the new church on December 12, 1926 and started to raise the $45.000 needed. The groundbreaking for the Byzantine brick structure took place in 1927 and the dedication was June 2, 1929, officiated by His Eminence, the Most Reverend Metropolitan Platon. St. Michael's now serves about 65 members. St. Michael's published a commemorative book for their recent 85th anniversary complete with congratulatory letters from the Mayor, the President and church officials.

SAINT NICHOLAS GREEK

Greek Orthodox
1931
4967 Forest Park
St. Louis, MO 63108

In 1904, a group of prominent St. Louis Hellenes organized Aghia Trias (Holy Trinity) as a Greek Church-Community. In 1906 , Reverend Panageotis Phiambolis was assigned by the Holy Synod of Greece as pastor of Holy Trinity Church as the first permanent Greek Orthodox priest in St. Louis. Shortly after the arrival of Father Phiambolis, a former Protestant church at 19th and Morgan (now Delmar) was rented for $50 a month. As a result of the dissatisfaction of some members of the Holy Trinity Church, the Church of Evangelismos was founded in 1910. They first met at a rented church at 17th and Olive in January of 1911. By 1917, the split factions of the Greek community came together and voted to organize a new church community, which was later named St. Nicholas. In October of 1917, a motion was passed to purchase an existing church and residence at Garrison and St. Louis avenues. This church was remodeled and was used by the St. Nicholas congregation until they moved to the present church in 1931. In September of 1918, the St. Louis Greek Community was one of three Greek Communities honored by a visit by His Beautitude, Meletios Metaxkis, Archbishop of the Autocephalous Church of Greece and subsequently Patriarch of Constantinople and Alexandria. On January 11, 1931, the cornerstone for the new St. Nicholas church was laid at the present site on Forest Park Blvd. The cost of the church was $132,315. Stained glass is by Emil Frei of St. Louis. In 1960-61, the church was expanded and remodeled at a cost of $490,000.

In 1919, the St. Nicholas Cemetery Committee purchased two acres of St. Matthew Cemetery. On May 30, 1949, a portion of that cemetery was designated as the American-Hellenic Memorial Cemetery in honor of the Greek war dead.

SAINT PAUL A.M.E.
African Methodist Episcopal
1891 (Formerly Hamilton Avenue Christian Church)
1260 Hamilton
St. Louis, MO 63112

The St. Paul African Methodist Episcopal Church was organized in 1841 and is the Oldest A.M.E. church west of the Mississippi river. It was formed under the leadership of Reverend William Paul Quinn, who had been sent from Philadelphia as a missionary of the A.M.E. Church. He was not permitted to preach in St. Louis upon his arrival as Missouri was a still slave state. The congregation originally met at a small log cabin near the end of Main Street, but soon moved to an old Presbyterian mission at Seventh and Washington. A new edifice was completed at Eleventh and Green streets in 1852. This was the first church built by St. Paul. By 1871, larger quarters were necessary and a brick structure was built. In 1890, the congregation moved to a new edifice at Lawton and Leffingwell streets. The new church was dedicated on the first Sunday in March, 1891. The congregation moved from their location at Lawton and Leffingwell on April 29, 1962. Robert H. Stockton, a member of the Hamilton Avenue Christian Church led the establishment of a number of Christian churches in the St. Louis area. Mr. Stockton's contributions to the Disciple related school in Canton, Missouri were so substantial that the name was changed to Culver Stockton College. Mrs. L.L. Culver was a friend of Mr. Stockton. The information from the original Hamilton Christian Church cornerstone has been destroyed or covered. The church now serves over 1300 members.

SAINT PAUL UNITED CHURCH OF CHRIST
United Church of Christ
1931 (Formerly St. Paul Evangelical & Reformed))
3510 Giles
St. Louis, MO 63116

The St. Paul Evangelical and Reformed congregation was organized in 1848 and their first church was built at 1808 South Ninth Street in 1850. A new church was built on the same site in 1874, but it was destroyed in the 1896 tornado. That church was replaced by the present building on that site in 1897. The St. Paul congregation moved to the location at Giles and Potomac in 1924 and by 1912, established a chapel on the site. As the congregation grew, a new church was required. It was designed by Hoener, Baum and Froese in brick and stone. The cornerstone was laid July 26, 1931 and the new church at Giles and Potomac dedicated May 15, 1932. The design is Gothic English Hall type. Stained glass is by Emil Frei, Jr. of Emil Frei Art Glass.

SAINT PAUL THE APOSTLE

Catholic
1937
4001 Jennings Road
St. Louis, MO 63121

SAINT PAUL'S EPISCOPAL

Episcopal
1848
10 East 3rd Street
Alton, IL 62002

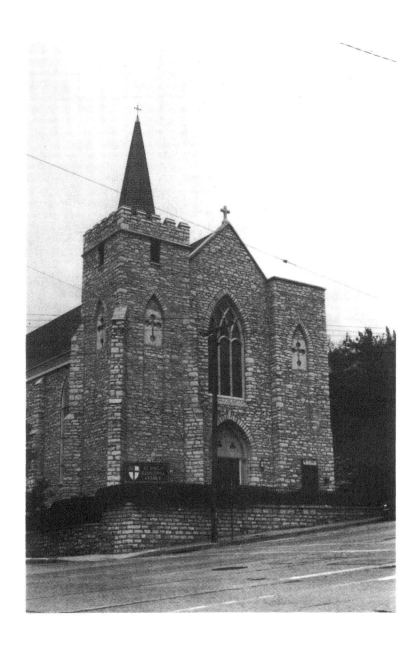

In 1834 Benjamin Godfrey arrived in Alton. Observing that the community had no church building, he provided the funds for the construction of a stone colonial church on the corner of Third and Market streets. He offered this church for the use of all organized religious groups. The Baptists, Episcopalians and Presbyterians used it regularly. As Captain Godfrey became a member of the Presbyterian Church, it became known as the Presbyterian Church. The Diocese of Illinois was created in 1835 and Alton Episcopalians elected their first vestry on February 20, 1836. In 1845 the Monticello Seminary, which now owned the church building, found itself in need of funds. The Presbyterians were expected to purchase it but hesitated. Captain Godfrey than offered it to the Episcopalians for $1800. The Vestry accepted the offer. Controversy arose over the bell which had been given to the First Presbyterian Church by Winthrop Gillman's mother. During the controversy, the bell was hauled away one night and now hangs in the tower of the First Presbyterian Church at Fourth and Alby. The Presbyterians reimbursed St. Paul's in the amount of $200. Bishop Chase consecrated St. Paul's on July 4, 1848.

By 1855 the congregation decided that a complete renovation of the church building was needed. Much of the old foundation was used, the walls were strengthened and 45 feet were added to the length of the building. The new structure was built at a cost of $10,000 and was consecrated by Bishop Whitehouse on July 4, 1857. Of interest, the congregation began calling their rector "Father" in 1925. Some members had used that form of address since the 1890's. The church was renovated by the parish in 1976.

SAINT PAUL'S LUTHERAN

Lutheran (Mo Synod)
1938
12345 Manchester
Des Peres, MO 63131

St. Paul's Lutheran congregation was formed in 1849 and met originally at the location of the cemetery on the west side of Ballas Road just South of Manchester. The present church designed by architects Wedemeyer, Cernik and Corrubia was built in 1938 of Wisconsin stone. An addition with new sanctuary was built in 1985 with stained glass by Emil Frei of St. Louis.

SAINT PAUL'S LUTHERAN

Lutheran
1926
2137 East John Avenue
St. Louis, MO 63107

The St. Paul's Lutheran congregation was formed in 1872 and met originally at Prairie and Von Phul streets. That church was destroyed by fire in 1922. The cornerstone for the present structure was laid in 1925 and the building finished February 7, 1926. The church is brick Gothic design. The building was heavily damaged by a fire December 26, 1990, but it was restored and rededicated on July 21, 1991. St. Paul's serves about 250 members.

SAINT PAUL'S METHODIST

United Methodist
1905
1927 St. Louis Avenue
St. Louis, MO 63106

St. Paul's Methodist Church is now closed. The windows have been removed or destroyed and most boarded up.

SAINT PAUL'S UNITED CHURCH OF CHRIST
United Church of Christ
1916 (Formerly St. Paul's Evangelical)
5508 Telegraph Road
St. Louis, MO 63129

SAINT PETER

Catholic
1861
324 South 3rd Street
St. Charles, MO 63301

On May 6, 1848, the first active resolution to organize the new German parish in St. Charles took place. Archbishop Kenrick granted permission to build the church and the cornerstone was laid on September 19, 1848 in honor of St. Peter, Prince of the Apostles. On March 25, 1861, a storm unroofed the entire building and damaged the interior. It was decided that a new and larger edifice would be built on the site and the cornerstone for the Romanesque style structure was laid June 13, 1861. In 1867, the bells, which are still in use were installed. A steeple, tower clock and organ were added in the 1870's. In 1909 it was decided that a new addition to the sanctuary would be built. The cornerstone for the new section was blessed May 22, 1910. The church was extensively renovated in 1944. In 1947, the organ, which had been in use since 1873, was replaced.

SAINT PETER & PAUL

Catholic
1873-1895
1919 South 7th Street
St. Louis, MO 63102
City Landmark: March, 1972

The year 1849 marks the founding of St. Peter & Paul's Parish. In that year the needs of a new German Parish, south of Carroll Street was greatly felt. Reverend Simon Sigrist, a young Theologian from Alsace, was called to organize the new parish. A lot was purchased from Mr. Allen at Eighth Street and Allen Avenue, upon which a one-story church was erected, facing Allen. This church soon proved too small for the growing congregation. They erected a brick church 90 feet long and 45 feet wide, which was dedicated by Coadjutor-Bishop Patrick Ryan, who later became Bishop of Philadelphia. The growth of the parish soon made erection of a larger church imperative. The cornerstone for the new structure was laid on April 12, 1874. The length of the church extends from Eighth to Seventh Street, a distance of 204 1/2 feet. The width of the transept is 87 feet. The height of the church is 70 feet. The tower measures 230 feet in height. The church was consecrated by Coadjutor Ryan on December 12, 1875. The church will seat 3000 people. On January 1, 1876, Father Goller announced that the last penny of the parish debt of $92,000 had been paid. The May 27, 1896 tornado damaged the church to the amount of $75,000. It was soon rebuilt.

The church is Norman Gothic of Grafton limestone and St. Genevieve sandstone trim and was designed by Franz George Himpler of New York. The painted stations of the cross in the church are from Beuron, Germany. The stained glass is from Innsbruck, Tyrol. Many years ago, the Quoins and Buttress facings were painted black, giving a definite identity to the church.

SAINT PETER & PAUL PARISH

Catholic
1855
717 State Street
Alton, IL 62002

St. Peter & Paul, formerly known as the Cathedral Church of Alton was built in 1855 and consecrated on May 15, 1859 by Archbishop Kenrick. It was the church of the new Diocese of Alton, which had been transferred from Quincy in 1857, when the new Bishop, Right Reverend Henry D. Juncker D.D. was named. In the early days, the Old Cathedral comprised a very large territory, including St. Patrick's and St. Mary's in Alton, St. Francis of Jerseyville, St. Mary's of Edwardsville and St. Patrick's of Grafton. The church is 125 feet long and 60 feet wide. In July, 1949 lightning struck the church. It shattered the organ and set fire to the steeples, which were destroyed. The church now serves about 2200 members in the Alton parish.

SAINT PETER'S A.M.E.

African Methodist Episcopal
Pre-1922 (Formerly Salem Evangelical)
4730 Margaretta
St. Louis, MO 63115

This church building, of red brick, formerly used by the Salem Evangelical, has had the cornerstone removed or covered so that the year of construction is unknown. The St. Peter's A.M.E. Church was organized in 1847 and was the second African Methodist church west of the Mississippi. The first church was erected on the corner of Elliot and Montgomery streets and consisted of two rooms. A second church on that site was destroyed in the 1927 tornado. The church moved to its present location at Margaretta and Shreve in 1962. In 1980, the church celebrated its 133rd anniversary by conducting a motorcade to the old church and taking the old cornerstone back to be installed in the present building. The congregation is associated with the outreach ministry and the J.R. Williams nursing unit.

SAINT PETER'S CATHEDRAL

Catholic
1870
200 West Harrison
Belleville, IL 62220

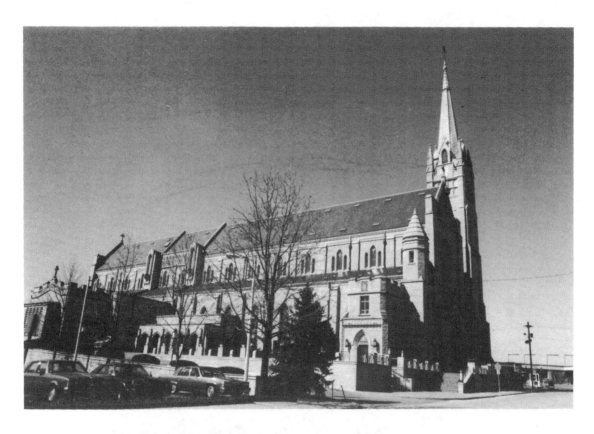

In 1834, the few Catholic families in Belleville erected a primitive frame church. In 1840, a larger church was erected of brick, east of the present one. The first resident priest was Reverend Casper Ostlangenberg. By 1869, it decided that a new and larger church was needed and it was soon built. It had barely been completed when faulty construction caused it to collapse and it had to be built over. In January of 1870, Father Baltes, the pastor of St. Peter's, was elected Bishop of Alton.

This Gothic Revival Cathedral was built in 1863. It was damaged by a fire and was rebuilt in 1912 by Victor J. Klutho. Extensive remodeling was accomplished in 1955-1969 by Paul J.Saunders.

SAINT PETER'S EPISCOPAL

Episcopal
1949
110 North Warson Road
St. Louis, MO 63124

St. Peter's Episcopal mission was founded in 1868 by Christ Church in a former skating rink on Olive near Compton. In 1872, it became part of St. Peter's Parish which was founded by Reverend Edward F. Berkley. The new church's first home was a hall at the northeast corner of Jefferson and Olive. This was used until a stone chapel was erected in 1873 at the northeast corner of Grand and Olive. Plans to erect a church on that lot were abandoned due to financial conditions and the congregation finally moved to Lindell and Spring. In 1949, the congregation moved to its present location at Ladue and Warson Roads. The building at Spring and Lindell has been destroyed. St. Peter's spawned the birth of four mission churches of St. Matthew's, St. Timothy's, Good Shepherd and St. Martin's.

SAINT PETER'S LUTHERAN

Lutheran (Mo Synod)
1925
1126 South Kingshighway
St. Louis, MO 63110

St. Peter's Lutheran Church was organized March 6, 1895 and met at Vista and Newstead, then later at Swan and Newstead. The cornerstone for the present church at Kingshighway and Wichita was laid February 5, 1925 and the building completed May 30, 1926.

SAINT PIUS V

Catholic
1916
3310 South Grand
St. Louis, MO 63118

St. Pius, in the southwestern part of the city was organized in 1905 by Reverend J. Lyons. A suitable location on the southeast corner of Grand Avenue and Utah Street was purchased, and a handsome combination church and school building was erected after the designs of Joseph Stauder & Sons, architects. The cornerstone for the present church, just north of the first one, was laid November 15, 1916 and consecrated on the Feast of the Most Holy Trinity on May 27, 1923. Some of the stained glass is by Emil Frei of St. Louis. In February of 1995, St. Pius V started offering a monthly mass for the many Vietnamese families of the South Grand parish.

SAINT ROCH'S

Catholic
1921
6052 Waterman
St. Louis, MO 63112

St. Roch's Parish was founded September 17, 1911. The cornerstone for the present church was laid September, 17, 1921 and the church completed in 1922. The Tudor Flemish Gothic church is built of brick and designed by architects Lee and Rush of St. Louis. Stained glass is by Emil Frei of St. Louis. The congregation serves about 350.

SAINT STANLISLAUS KOSTKA

Catholic
1891
1413 North 20th Street
St. Louis, MO 63106
National Historic Register: July 10, 1979
City Landmark: March, 1976

What was formerly the heart of "Kerry Patch" was transformed into a most respectable neighborhood. The transformation was caused by the location of St. Stanlislaus Parish in that vicinity. In 1882, Reverend Urban Stankowski was charged with the organization of the first Polish parish in St. Louis. Plans for the new church were soon drawn by architect Louis Wessbecher of Wessbecher & Hummel of St. Louis. The red brick and stone structure, built in the shape of a Greek cross was built at a cost of $90,000. The cornerstone was laid in 1891 and when completed, St. Stanislaus soon became the mother-church of the Poles in St. Louis. The church serves about 285 families today.

SAINT STEPHEN UNITED CHURCH OF CHRIST

United Church of Christ
1938
8500 Halls Ferry
St. Louis, MO 63147

St. Stephen was organized March 20, 1896 as a German congregation serving railroad car craftsmen, truck farmers and shop keepers. The original location was at Halls Ferry and Gimblin. German language services were held until World War I when English became the predominate language. The groundbreaking for the present building was in March of 1936 and the new church in Williamsburg Colonial Brick was dedicated in September of 1938. The architects were Manske & Dieckman of St. Louis. St. Stephen serves about 420 members today.

SAINT STEPHEN'S EVANGELICAL LUTHERAN

Lutheran
1894 (Formerly St. George's Episcopal)
515 Pendleton
St. Louis, MO 63108

After their previous church was destroyed by fire in 1891, St. George's Episcopal Church decided to move west to Olive and Pendleton. The architect Kivas Tulley was commissioned to design an impressive new church but the financial panic of 1893 prevented it from being built. It was then decided to construct a smaller, less expensive church on the same site. The new cornerstone was laid and the new church built in 1894. By 1913, St. George had combined with the church of St. Michael and All Angels and the congregation moved to the present site at Wydown and Ellenwood in what was known as Skinker Heights. The church is now the home of St. Stephen's Lutheran.

SAINT TERESA OF AVILA

Catholic
1900
3636 North Market
St. Louis, MO 63113

St. Teresa's Parish was organized in 1865 by Reverend Father James O'Brien. He was succeeded after one year by Reverend Francis P. Gallagher, under who's leadership the first church was erected. By 1892, the parish had grown to about 300 families and a new church became necessary. The cornerstone of the new edifice at Grand and North Market was laid on Pentecost Sunday, June 3, 1900, by Bishop Montgomery of Los Angeles, who acted in the absence of Archbishop J.J. Kain who was in Rome at that time. The new stone church was dedicated by Archbishop Kain on October 6, 1901.

SAINT THOMAS AQUIN

Catholic
1882
3949 Iowa
St. Louis, MO 63118

St. Anthony's Parish, administered by the Franciscan Fathers, was organized in 1862 as a "mixed" parish, and remained so for twenty years. In 1882, owing to the crowded condition at St. Anthony's, the English speaking parishioners separated and organized a congregation under the name of St. Thomas of Aquin, with Reverend David J. Dougherty as the first pastor. A neat church was built at Iowa and Osage streets, its cornerstone laid October 9, 1882 and the dedication held on April 30, 1883. The church is red brick in Gothic style and is 74 by 48 feet in size. The tower was damaged in the May 27, 1896 tornado and was capped off with bulbous, curving roof. The church owns a copy of Murillo's "St. Thomas of Aquin" contracted by F.O. Broehne.

SAINT TRINITY LUTHERAN

Lutheran (Mo Synod)
1870
7404 Vermont Avenue
St. Louis, MO 63111
Carondelet Historical

St. Trinity Church near Koeln and Vermont was built in 1870-72 of red brick. St. Trinity was at that time a German Evangelical Lutheran congregation which was formed June 21, 1859. The church now serves about 180 members.

SAINT VINCENT DE PAUL

Catholic
1845
1417 South 9th Street
St. Louis, MO 63104
City Landmark: March, 1971

In 1839, Reverend John Timon, C.M., later bishop of Buffalo, New York, was charged with the organization of a parish in south St. Louis to be placed in charge of the Vicentian Fathers in connection with the Diocesan seminary. A lot in the block bounded by Marion, Carroll, Eighth and Ninth streets was donated, upon which the erection of a new church was begun. On April 9, 1839, the cornerstone was laid by Bishop Rosati and the church was dedicated in honor of the "Holy Trinity." A low row of frame buildings was also erected, called "Bishop's Row," in which the seminary was located. services in Holy Trinity were held in English, French and German. In was soon decided that a new church was needed and it would be built on land purchased from Mrs. Soulard for $12,000. The cornerstone was laid March 17, 1844 and the church was consecrated by Archbishop Kenrick on November 1, 1845. St. Vincent de Paul was designed by London trained architect George I. Barnett, then in the firm of Meriwether Lewis Clark, the son of Captain William Clark. The brick and stone church is of Renaissance/Romanesque design and is 64 by 150 feet. The narthex and facade are by Franz Saler and were done in 1849. A Pfeffer organ, made nearby on Marion Street in 1874, still serves the congregation.

SAINT WENCESLAUS

Catholic
1936
3014 Oregon
St. Louis, MO 63118

Through the efforts of the Very Reverend Msgr. Joseph Hessoun, St. Wenceslaus Parish was organized in 1894, as the second Bohemian church in St. Louis. Its first pastor was Reverend B.H. Faitlik. By 1910, the parish numbered about 120 families. St. Wenceslaus was the King of Bohemia. The present church structure was built on the same site in 1936. Some of the stained glass is by Emil Frei of St. Louis. St. Wenceslaus supports the St. Louis Byzantine Mission which is a group of Catholics who are determined to keep their Eastern Rite Mass form intact. This liturgy is celebrated every Sunday ta 6:00 p.m. at St. Wenceslaus. Permission has been given from Rome to celebrate the mass in both rites. The rite also serves to educate local Roman Catholics about the Byzantine rites.

SALEM LUTHERAN

Lutheran (Mo Synod)
1951
8343 Gravois Road
St. Louis, MO 63123

Salem Lutheran Church was founded in 1909, the small congregation meeting in the summer kitchen of the Dietrich Wilke family on Weber Road. The first services were conducted by Reverend Otto Laskowski of Concordia Lutheran in Maplewood. Salem's first church was on donated land at 5031 Lakewood Avenue. The minutes of the meeting, written in German, specified the new building to be 26 by 48 feet. Its total cost was to be $2,200. The name of the new church was "Salem Evangelical Lutheran Congregation of the Unaltered Augsburg Confession." Groundbreaking for Salem's new building took place on July 10, 1949 with the dedication on December 2, 1951. The cost of this new church was more than $256,000. The building is Limestone and rock in Modified Gothic design by Ted Steinmeyer. Today, Salem serves more than 2,300.

SALEM LUTHERAN

Lutheran (Mo Synod)
1899
5180 Parker Road
Florissant, MO 63033

Between 1839 and 1849 a small number of Lutherans left their homes in Bielefeld, Germany and arrived in St. Louis. These Germans began worshipping in the area they called New Bielfeld in their native tongue and in November, 1848, Salem Evangelical Church of New Bielefeld was organized with Reverend C.H. Schliepsick as the first pastor. A one room log church was completed in 1851, replaced in 1861 by a larger brick structure. This church was built from hand made bricks and stones from a local quarry. In 1876 a German newcomer from Bielefeld brought a gift of a bell cast in Bielefeld. The church had no tower so the bell was hung in a wooden tower in the church yard. The bell survives and is still used today in the present church. Bricks for the present church were hauled by horse and wagon from the chain of Rocks Road and the new church was dedicated on November 12, 1899. The area of New Bielefeld was now called Black Jack. The church is Gothic design with brick and quarried stone. In 1993, the church was restored and remodeled, adding an addition to the front and narthex. The renovation work was designed by Manske & Diekman architects of St. Louis. The white brick church school house across the road from Salem church was built in 1895 and is a St. Louis County Historic building.

SALEM IN BALLWIN UMC

United Methodist
1870
1482 Manchester Road
Ballwin, MO 63011
National Historic Register

When John Ball laid out the town of Ballwin in 1837, he chose one block as a site for a meeting house for the Methodist Episcopal Congregation (St. Louis German Conference for the ME Church), and a second block for a burying ground. A few families met in their homes and were visited by Methodist circuit riders. Between visits, they continued to hold meetings in their home.

In 1846, Reverend Henry Koeneke, Sr., District Superintendent of the St. Louis District, sent Reverend

H. Hohmann to be the first preacher. The founding of the congregation was in 1847, when the group secured its seal of organization. By 1855, the congregation erected a small white frame building, not far from the present location. The first and only school in Ballwin from 1855 to 1869 was conducted by the church in the church building. In 1869, the Board of Education, District 45, bought the building from the church for $800. The church reserved the right to conduct its services there until the new church could be built. The present brick sanctuary was constructed in 1870 at a cost of $4,500. It was built with bricks furnished by Mr. Kessler. These bricks were made by his slaves at what is now known as the "Barn at Lucerne." This brick sanctuary has been in use constantly since 1870 and remains exactly as it was built. Until World War I, the German language was the prominent language. By 1961 the membership had grown to 575 members. Under the guidance of Church Extension, Etc., the church agreed to support a new Methodist Church in Ellisville, Missouri and almost 100 active members left to start this new church.

SCRUGGS MEMORIAL CME

Christian Methodist Episcopal
1906 (Formerly Cook Avenue Methodist Episcopal, South)
3860 Cook Avenue
St. Louis, MO 63113

This church was built originally around 1906 for the Sunday School mission of St. John's Methodist Episcopal Church South. The church was organized with only six members in 1877. In 1879, another member of St. John's joined the church. This was Richard M. Scruggs, a St. Louis businessman. He was elected Superintendent of the Sunday School. When the congregation was at the point of needing a new structure for worship bigger than the frame house at 3700 Page, $35,000 was raised by subscriptions and was matched by Mr. Scruggs as a gift. The new building was erected at the corner of Cook and Spring avenues and was officially named Cook Avenue Methodist Episcopal Church, South. By 1925, the neighborhood was changing and the structure was sold to the African Methodist Episcopal Church. In August of 1950, the old cornerstone with original information was removed and a new one naming the church Scruggs Memorial C.M.E. was laid. The original congregation used the money from the sale to build a new church for the Grand Avenue Methodist Episcopal Church, renamed the Richard M. Scruggs Memorial United Methodist Church.

SECOND PRESBYTERIAN

Presbyterian (USA)
1899
4501 Westminster Place
St. Louis, MO 63108
National Historic Register: September 11, 1975
City Landmark: September, 1973

The site at Westminster Place and Taylor Avenue is the third location of Second Presbyterian Church founded in 1838. From 1840 to 1870 it was housed in a Greek Revival structure at Fifth and Walnut streets. In 1870 it relocated to the western end of Lucas Place at Seventeenth Street. In 1896 the first building on Westminster, the chapel was completed. Morning services were held there until late in 1900 when the sanctuary was dedicated. The chapel and sanctuary are Richardsonian Romanesque Revival style with the chapel designed by Shepley, Rutan and Coolidge. By 1899 the Shepley firm was no longer active in St. Louis and the church turned to Theodore C. Link of St. Louis to design the sanctuary. Link is best known for his work on Union Station in 1894. In addition to the exterior design the interior is enhanced by the beauty of the stained glass windows; 13 by Louis Comfort Tiffany, 1900-1922, 2 by Emil Frei, 1930-1955, 1 by Rodney Winfield, 1 by Charles Connick, 1930 and 2 of unknown origin (Probably Church Cut Glass & Decorating of Chicago, 1910)

The years following World War II brought a declining neighborhood and loss of membership as members moved to the suburbs. After unsuccessful attempts to find another location the congregation voted in 1961 to stay on its corner and become a city church. The church was renovated in 1985-87 by Kurt Lanberg of St. Louis., an effort that was completely paid for by 1990

SHAARE EMETH

Jewish
1931 (Formerly Shaare Emeth)
6890 Delmar
University City, MO 63130

Shaare Emeth (Gates of Truth) was organized in 1866 by a group of Reform Jews who had been meeting since 1863 and became the first Reform congregation in St. Louis. They built a large, twin spired synagogue at 17th and Pine, dedicating it in 1869. The first Rabbi was Dr. Solomon H. Sonnenschein, who led the congregation to become the leading Reform congregation west of the Mississippi. In 1895, Shaare Emeth moved to a large stone temple at the southeast corner of Lindell and Vandeventer. The congregation remained at Lindell until 1929, when it became necessary to raze the temple because of the widening of Vandeventer Avenue. The old Egyptian building at the southeast corner of Trinity & Delmar in University City was purchased and razed. The new temple, designed by Alfred S. Alschuler of Chicago, was dedicated in 1932 and was the first Jewish congregation in St. Louis County. Rabbi Julius Gordon later said that the Egyptian building was destroyed because "The Jews couldn't go back to Egypt after the Exodus." Shaare Emeth has since moved to 11645 Ladue Road in West County. The building is now the home of the St. Louis Symphony Music School.

SHILOH TEMPLE

Church of God in Christ
1888 (Formerly First Presbyterian)
4100 Washington
St. Louis, MO 63108

Reverend Salmon Giddings arrived in St. Louis April 5, 1816 as a recently ordained Congregational minister from Connecticut. By August of 1816, Giddings organized his first congregation, a Presbyterian Church at Bellevue, eighty miles south of St. Louis. Two months later he organized the Bonhomme Presbyterian Church on Conway Road. By 1817, he organized the First Presbyterian Church with only ten members, but those members included such notable people as Alexander McNair, the first Governor of Missouri and Thomas Hart Benton, one of the first senators from Missouri. Many problems kept the first church from being completed, but in 1825, the first Protestant church in St. Louis was dedicated. Revered Giddings served as the church's pastor from 1826 until he died in 1828. The First Presbyterian Church took Reverend Giddings body with them when the moved to various locations, but he is now at rest at the Bonhomme Church cemetery in west St. Louis County. In 1888, the First Presbyterian Church moved into this stone structure at 4100 Washington Avenue. First Presbyterian Church was a supporter of the abolitionist movement before the Civil War, so some members favoring slavery left and formed what is now the Memorial Presbyterian Church on Skinker.

SHILOH UNITED METHODIST

United Methodist
1875
210 South Main
Shiloh, IL 62002
St. Clair County Historical Landmark
D.A.R. Historical

The Shiloh Methodist Church was organized August 6, 1807 by Bishop McKendree and Reverend Jesse Walker. A log cabin was built August 10, 1807 on the site where three springs met. The Missouri Conference was organized here in 1816 and met here in 1820.

SHINING LIGHT TABERNACLE

Full Gospel
1891 (Formerly Deutches Evangelische Christus Kirche)
7121 Manchester Road
St. Louis, MO 63143
City Landmark: September, 1978

The Christ Evangelical Church was dedicated in early 1891 as a sister congregation to St. Mark's Evangelical Church at Jefferson and Potomac. The congregation moved from this little white church in 1919 to the present location at Bellevue and Bruno in Maplewood. This building was later owned by a Church of the Nazerene congregation and is now Full Gospel.

SOLOMON'S TEMPLE

Non-Denominational
1909 (Formerly 4th Church of Christ, Scientist)
5569 Page Blvd.
St. Louis, MO 63112

SOUTHERN MISSION BAPTIST

Missionary Baptist
1911-1941 (Formerly Winstanley Baptist)
2801 State Street
East St. Louis, IL 62201

The organization of Winstanley Baptist came about from the idea of Pastor Adam Faucett of the First Baptist Church in East St. Louis. The church had its beginnings as a Sunday School in the school building of the Winstanley Park School at the southwest corner of 27th and Henrietta. The group moved soon to 26th Street north of State and the church was formed there, September 8, 1907. Winstanley was started the same year as the Illinois Baptist State Association. The name Winstanley came from the landowner Thomas Winstanley who owned the property where the church was formed. At one time, Winstanley Park was a separate community unto itself. The property at 28th and State street upon which the church building stands was purchased on October 11, 1911. Because the church had little money, the first building on this site was built from cobblestones that were hauled from State Street when the streetcar tracks were installed. The outside walls of the building were made from these cobblestones. The church became known as the "Rock Church".

In 1933 an educational building was added to the rear of the original unit consisting of a basement and two floors. In 1941 the building was enlarged by building a new entrance and balcony, and increasing the seating capacity of the auditorium. The cornerstone for this part of the building was laid on December 7, 1941 and contains items of interest concerning the church and its people. In 1956, a brick veneer was built on the 28th Street wall of the church. Due to changes in the area, the Winstanley Baptist Church has since moved to Fairview Heights to carry on its traditions. The old church building is now occupied by the Southern Mission Missionary Baptist Church.

SOUTHSIDE FREE WILL BAPTIST

Baptist
1894 (Formerly Trinity Evangelical, Southside Church of Christ)
4600 Michigan
St. Louis, MO 63111

STARLIGHT BAPTIST

Baptist
Pre-1880 (Unknown)
2347 Sullivan
St. Louis, MO 63106

Although this structure served as a sheet iron works as early as 1896 and later saw service as a shade factory, it was apparently built as a church. The original congregation is unknown. It is now the home of the Starlight Baptist Church. There is no cornerstone or construction information available, but the design of the building indicates German heritage.

THIRD PRESBYTERIAN

Presbyterian (USA)
1915
2426 Union Blvd.
St. Louis, MO 63113

TRANSFORMATION CHRISTIAN

Christian
1897 (Formerly St. Ann's Catholic)
4100 Page Blvd.
St. Louis, MO 63113

The origin of St. Ann's Parish was an attempt to organize a parish under the title of St. Paul the Apostle on Finney Avenue, a few blocks west of Grand. Reverend John Tuohy was the pastor. He was succeeded by Reverend O.S. McDonald, who, finding the location unsuitable, established the church at Page Boulevard and Whittier Street and the name was changed to St. Ann's. The cornerstone of the new church was laid by Archbishop J.J. Kain, on May 9, 1897, on the Feast of the Patronage of St. Joseph. The church, designed by Barnett, Haynes and Barnett, was finally dedicated and blessed by Archbishop John Glennon on May 13, 1910. It cost about $60,000. Emil Frei, Sr. created the stained glass. The structure is now the home of the Transformation Christian Church. St. Ann's Parish merged with Visitation on September 23, 1992.

TRINITY EPISCOPAL

Episcopal
1899-1910 (Formerly St. James & Our Redeemer)
600 North Euclid
St. Louis, MO 63108

TRINITY LUTHERAN

Lutheran (Mo Synod)
1897
1805 South 8th Street
St. Louis, MO 63104

Formed in 1839 by a group of Saxon-Germans seeking religious freedom, Trinity is the oldest Lutheran congregation west of the Mississippi River. They met originally in the Christ Episcopal Church at Broadway and Chestnut. The congregation moved to this location from a site farther northeast near the river at Third and Lombard. The original 1864 building, destroyed in the 1896 tornado, was replaced with the current Eclectic American Gothic structure. The present red brick church was dedicated March 28, 1897. Trinity Lutheran School has been holding classes since 1839 and is recognized as the oldest continuously operating elementary school in the St. Louis area. Through the efforts of its pastor, Carl F. W. Walther, Trinity was instrumental in forming the Lutheran Church, Missouri Synod.

TRINITY PRESBYTERIAN

Presbyterian (USA)
1922
6800 Washington
St. Louis, MO 63130

TRINITY TEMPLE PENTECOST

Pentecost
1897 (Formerly Zion Methodist Episcopal)
7427 Virginia Avenue
St. Louis, MO 63111

TRINITY UNITED CHURCH OF CHRIST

United Church of Christ
1930 (Formerly Trinity Evangelical)
4700 South Grand
St. Louis, MO 63111

TYLER PLACE PRESBYTERIAN

Presbyterian (USA)
1901
2109 Spring Avenue
St. Louis, MO 63110

Tyler Place Presbyterian Church was organized December 14, 1896. The cornerstone for this structure was laid January 1, 1901. In 1946, the Lafayette Park Presbyterian Church merged with the Tyler Place Church.

UNION AVENUE CHRISTIAN

Christian
1904
733 Union
St. Louis, MO 63108
City Landmark: November, 1974

The original Church was organized in 1871 after some members of the Central Christian Church were dismissed when they insisted that instrumental music had a place in religious services. In 1875, they relocated to 23rd and Washington. In 1902, Mount Cabanne Christian united with the Central group and formed the Union Avenue Christian Church. This building was built in 1904. The Italian Romanesque structure of smooth and rough cut stone was designed by Weber & Groves with an addition in 1907 by Albert B. Groves of St. Louis. The name of Union Avenue was changed to Union Boulevard in 1882.

UNION METHODIST EPISCOPAL

Methodist
1884 (Formerly First Congregational , Union Methodist Episcopal)
3610 Grandel Square
St. Louis, MO 63108

In the 1880's, the area known as "Piety Hill" in Stoddard's Addition had at least seven churches. One of these was the Union Methodist located on the southwest corner of Garrison and Lucas from 1882 to 1915 This church was an outgrowth of Ebenezer Chapel, the city's first Methodist church, disbanded in 1861 because of the northern sympathy of its members in a pro-southern denomination. In 1862, the congregation was re-organized as the Union Methodist Church and moved into the former Union Presbyterian Church at 11th and Locust. During the civil War, a large American flag flew from its tower, with an armed guard posted at the entrance. The church moved to the Garrison Avenue location in 1882, but that church was destroyed by fire in 1911. The structure was rebuilt, but the congregation moved to 3610 Grandel Square and purchased the First Congregational Church. Union Methodist remained at this location until 1952 when it merged with Christ Methodist and occupied a new building at 3543 Watson Road. In 1953, the Grandel building was sold to a Pentecostal congregation. The building now houses the St. Louis Black Repertory Theater.

UNION PROTESTANT

Various Protestant
1895-1900
646 rue St. Francois
Florissant, MO 63031
National Historic Register
Florissant Landmark

The history of this chapel dates to about 1857 when the property was entrusted to several people with the instructions to erect a "good, substantial and finished house of worship" for the use of all of the protestants of St. Ferdinand. In particular, it was to be used by the Methodists and Presbyterians. When the church was finally built, it was called the Union Protestant Church. In 1948, the church was purchased by the Florissant Presbyterian Church. This congregation extensively remodeled and improved the structure. In 1959, it was sold to Trinity Missionary Baptist Church. By 1972, it was being used by Faith Tabernacle Full Gospel Church. The church is now called Old Town Chapel and is used for wedding services with an area for receptions downstairs. It will seat about 150 people in the sanctuary.

UNITED HEBREW TEMPLE

Jewish
1924-27 (Formerly United Hebrew Temple)
225 South Skinker Blvd.
St. Louis, MO 63105

In 1840, Heidelberg, Germany native Louis Bomeisler and others bought a piece of ground for $205 and in 1841, formed the first Jewish congregation in St. Louis. They called their congregation United Hebrew. Bomeisler was a graduate of Heidelberg University and spoke seven languages. He was sent as a diplomat to the Congress of Vienna in 1814 and became an aide-de-camp to one of Napoleons generals. The new United Hebrew congregation first met at the Oracle Coffee House near Second and Locust streets to draw up a constitution, agreeing to abide by all Jewish traditions. When United Hebrew decided to build a synagogue, they appealed to the populace to contribute because of the support that the "Israelites" had given to many local public ventures. The public responded and the new building at 420 North Sixth Street was dedicated on June 17, 1859. United Hebrew's building was used by the Third Baptist Church, the First Christian Church and the St. George Episcopal Church during periods of transition to new buildings. United Hebrew changed to Reform Judaism early in its life. From 1880 to 1903, United Hebrew congregation was located at the southwest corner of 21st and Olive streets. In 1903, they moved to Kingshighway and Enright. This Temple at 225 South Skinker was occupied in 1926. In 1991, the structure was dedicated as the new library for the Missouri Historical Society. The interior renovation, directed by Attorney and St. Louis Landmarks Association member H. Mead Summers, not only restored the original glory of the building, but improved on it in many ways. Mr. Summers exceptional sense of color and design have enhanced the building's original architecture. The United Hebrew congregation is now located in west St. Louis County.

UNIVERSITY UNITED METHODIST

United Methodist
1925
6901 Washington
St. Louis, MO 63130

The University Methodist congregation was organized in 1914. The church at Washington and Trinity was designed by architect Albert B. Groves and the cornerstone was laid in 1925.

VISITATION ST. ANN'S SHRINE

Catholic
1909 (Formerly Visitation Catholic)
4515 Evans (Taylor and MLK)
St. Louis, MO 63113

The parish of the Visitation was organized in 1881 by Reverend Edward Fenlon. A temporary church was built and a school and rectory provided for. Father Fenlon was succeeded by Father Edward J. Dempsey in December of 1898. The Gothic/Basilica church without transept, designed by architects Barnett, Haynes & Barnett was built in 1909 of red brick and stone. On September 23, 1992, St. Ann's church closed and the congregation merged with Visitation to become Visitation-St. Ann's Shrine. Visitation is recognized as the first integrated Catholic Church in St. Louis.

WASHINGTON TABERNACLE

Baptist
1876 (Formerly Walnut Street Presbyterian, Washington-Compton
Presbyterian)
3200 Washington Blvd.
St. Louis, MO 63103
City Landmark: April, 1984

The Washington-Compton Presbyterian Church occupied the large stone edifice at that intersection from 1880 to 1926. It began as a mission of the Second Church in 1859 and the congregation erected a church at 16th and Walnut which was leased from 1860 to 1862 by the Union Presbyterian, formerly at Eleventh and Locust. In 1864, the congregation was called the Walnut Street Presbyterian Church. In 1880, they moved to the Washington-Compton location and the name was changed to Washington-Compton Presbyterian Church. In 1926, the church moved to Skinker Blvd. and Alexander Drive and adopted its present name of Memorial Presbyterian. The Washington Avenue building was renovated in 1948 and is now occupied by the Washington Tabernacle Baptist Church which was formed in 1902. This church was the site of Dr. Martin Luther King's Civil Rights Rally in May of 1963. The church was designed by John Maurice and Charles K. Ramsey and built of white stone. The original cornerstone has been removed or covered, but the present congregation is aware of the church's history.

WAY OF LIFE CHURCH

Non-Denominational
1891 (Formerly Marvin Memorial Methodist, South)
2526 South 12th Street
St. Louis, MO 63104

The Marvin Methodist Episcopal, South Mission was organized in a blacksmith shop in 1859 and later used rented rooms for services. In 1874, a frame mission building was dedicated at 2629 Menard Street. The mission was organized as the Marvin Methodist Episcopal Church, South in 1875. The present building was erected in 1891 at 1129 Sidney Street. The church was later known as the Marvin Memorial Methodist Church. The structure is now the home of the Way of Life Outreach Ministry and the address has been changed to 2526-30 South Twelfth Street.

WAYMAN A.M.E

African Methodist Episcopal
1908 (Formerly Kingshighway Cumberland Presbyterian)
5010 Cabanne
St. Louis, MO 63113

This structure was originally the home of the Kingshighway Cumberland Presbyterian Church. The original cornerstone has been removed or covered so the history of the previous congregation is unknown.

WEBSTER HILLS UNITED METHODIST

United Methodist
1931
698 West Lockwood
Webster Groves, MO 63119

Dr. Franklin Fillmore Lewis was the founder of the Webster Hills United Methodist Church. He was District Superintendent of the Methodist Episcopal Church of the area and obtained the three lots on which the present church is built. Edward W. Potts was appointed as the first pastor by Bishop Lynn Waldorf. On September 7, 1930, the first Sunday school and church services were held in the Henry Hough School in Glendale. The cornerstone for the chapel was laid September 13, 1931. The first service was held April 10, 1932. In September 1953, the congregation decided to build a new sanctuary. The cornerstone was laid September 11, 1955 and the structure consecrated September 16, 1956 along with the dedication of the Franklin F. Lewis Chapel, which is the old sanctuary.

WEBSTER PRESBYTERIAN

Presbyterian
1891-1924
45 West Lockwood
Webster Groves, MO 63119

WESTMINSTER PRESBYTERIAN

Presbyterian (USA)
1916
5300 Delmar
St. Louis, MO 63112
City Landmark: November, 1974

Westminster Presbyterian Church began life in 1853 as the Pine Street Church, which was located at Eleventh and Pine. The church moved to a chapel on Grand Boulevard opposite Washington Avenue in 1880. At that time, the church name was changed to Grand Avenue Church and the cornerstone for the new building was laid in 1882. The $145,000 church was built of rough cut limestone in Gothic style and had gable ends each 100 feet in height. It was occupied until 1914 when the church moved to a chapel at the present site at Union and Delmar. The old church was converted into a movie theater and was razed when the Fox theater was being built in 1927. The present structure of English Gothic Bedford limestone in Scotch ashlar with Caen stone interior facings was designed in 1916 by Albert B. Groves of St. Louis. Groves also designed the oak interior trim and collaborated with Marx & Jones to design the windows. Additionally, some of the windows from the Grand Avenue church were incorporated into the new building.

ZION LUTHERAN

Lutheran (Mo Synod)
1894
2500 North 21st Street
St. Louis, MO 63106

Zion Evangelical Lutheran Church was founded April 6, 1860 and began worshipping in a building at Blair and Warren streets. Zion was one of the first four congregations joined in a "Generalgeneinde" or united congregation under the leadership of Dr. C.F.W. Walther, the first president of the Lutheran Church-Missouri Synod and president of Concordia Seminary of St. Louis. In 1894, Zion bought land on Benton Street and built the present church building for $50,000. The new church was dedicated on December 22, 1895. The altar is made of Italian marble and is flanked by figures of Moses and Paul. The lectern and pulpit are also of marble, the pulpit decorated with images of the four Gospel writers; Matthew, Mark, Luke and John. The structure is French Gothic and was designed by an architect named Knell.

The Emil Frei Art Glass Company

The firm of Emil Frei, Inc., founded in St. Louis in 1900 and still operating today, has been one of the leading companies in the field of stained glass and mosaics in the United States. Founded by Bavarian-born artist, Emil Frei, Sr. (1869-1942), Emil Frei, Inc. has remained a traditional-style association of craftsmen and artists under the leadership of three generations of Freis, each of whom has made and overseen major artistic contributions to the field of stained glass and/or mosaic design, especially in the realm of the liturgical arts.

Emil Frei, Sr., was born in Bavaria in 1869 and studied at the Munich Academy of Art. Upon completion of his studies he emigrated to New York to escape the universal military service then required in Germany. There he was joined by his fiance' Emma Mueller of Heidelberg, whom he soon married. Shortly thereafter the Freis moved to San Francisco where Emil, Sr. worked as a mural painter. In 1898, Emil Frei was invited to come to St. Louis to undertake the design and execution of stained glass for a large new church then under construction. This project, the stained glass windows for the St. Francis Xavier (College) Church at 239 North Grand, did not, however, come to fruition until a generation later when it was undertaken by Frei's son and successor, Emil Frei, Jr.

Emil Frei, Sr. was initially employed in St. Louis as an artist for A.H. Wallis. In 1900, he opened his own stained glass company, Emil Frei Art Glass, Co., at 19 South Broadway. In 1903 the business moved to 3715 California Avenue, and then in 1907 to 3934 South Grand, where it remained until 1972. Emil Frei was assisted in these early years by his wife Emma, who served at varying times as vice-president, treasurer and secretary of Emil Frei Art Glass, Co., until her retirement in 1930.

The Emil Frei Art Glass, Co., specializing in Munich antique glass figured style windows, grew quickly. By 1909 the company employed fifteen artists and nine glassblowers in studios in Munich and St. Louis. Windows designed for the Holy Family Church in Watertown, New York, won grand prize at the 1904 Louisiana Purchase Exposition.

It was in the field of mosaic design, however, where Emil Frei, Sr., made his best remembered contribution to liturgical art. In the 1920's he was commissioned to design the mosaics for the new st. Louis Cathedral on Lindell Boulevard. To undertake this project, Emil Frei, in conjunction with the Berlin art glass and mosaic firm of Puhl u. Wagner, founded Ravenna Mosaics, In. (later known as The Ravenna Company), in 1924. Until 1929 there was little distinction between Ravenna Mosaics and Emil Frei Art Glass. The companies shared quarters at the latter's South Grand location, and Emil Frei and his wife Emma occupied the respective offices of president and vice-president in both firms. In 1929 Ravenna Mosaics separated from Emil Frei Art Glass and moved to New York for a period of ten years. Upon its return to St. Louis in 1939, the Ravenna Company, now under the leadership of Paul Heudeck, again shared quarters with Emil Frei, In., until the end of World War II when it moved to its own location at 5205-09 South Grand.

In 1930, after the departure of Ravenna Mosaics, Inc. for New York, The Emil Frei Art Glass, Co., re-organized as Emil Frei, Inc. Emil Frei., Sr. remained president, Emma Frei retired as vice-president in favor of her son, Emil Frei, Jr., and Julius Gewinner became treasurer. Both Julius Gewinner and Emil Frei, Jr., had joined Emil Frei Art Glass as artists in 1917. Gewinner moved into the business end of the operation, becoming a department manager in 1926 and production manager in 1927. From 1930 until his retirement in 1968 he served as treasurer, and after the death of Emil Frei, Sr., in 1942, he also assumed the duties of vice-president. Gewinner's extended tenure as treasurer and later vice-president, helped give Emil Frei, Inc., a remarkable degree of continuity.

Emil Frei, Jr., was the other pillar of the firm between 1930 and his death in 1967. Born in 1896, he studied art at Washington University before joining his father's firm in 1917. Throughout the 1920's and 1930's he exerted a significant artistic influence within Emil Frei, Inc., as he worked to recreate the vivid and colorful 13th century medallion style stained glass windows like those at the Cathedral of Chartres. It fell to him to design the windows at St. Francis Xavier (College) Church in St. Louis, a project that did much to build his reputation as one of the foremost designers of stained glass in the United States. After his father's death in 1942, Emil Frei, Jr., assumed the presidency of Emil Frei, Inc., retaining that office until 1963, when he became chairman of the board until his death in 1967.

Under the leadership of Emil Frei, Jr., Emil Frei, Inc. rose to even greater heights as a new generation of artists associated with the firm and brought new techniques and different artistic perspectives to the stained glass medium. Due in part to the disruption of World War II and the subsequent liquidation of Emil Frei, Inc's., assets in Germany, the focus shifted from the German figure style window produced in the Munich studio to the modernistic and often abstract stained glass windows designed by the company's St. Louis based artists. The first modern windows were designed by Robert Harmon, who joined Emil Frei, Inc., in 1938, and remained with the company until his retirement in 1968. Harmon was responsible for some of the most innovative and creative windows and mosaics that came out of Emil Frei, Inc., during the post World War II years. From the end of World War II through the 1960's, the work of artists Francis Deck, Milton Frenzel, William Schickel, Joan Velligan, Rodney Winfield and Siegfried Reinhardt stood along side that of Harmon as pioneering efforts in the stained glass medium and in the realm of mosaic, mural and sculpture design as well. In addition, Emil Frei, Jr's., son, Robert Frei, who joined the company as an artist in 1946, exerted comparable influence.

in 1963 Robert Frei assumed the presidency of Emil Frei, Inc., and ran the company under the tutelage of his father. During the beginning of Robert Frei's presidency, the firm began to seek new and more varied outlets for the stained glass medium, experimenting with more new techniques and the use of stained glass in secular as well as religious contexts. After the death of Emil Frei, Jr., in 1967, and following the retirement of Julius Gewinner and Robert

Harmon shortly thereafter, an era came to an end. Nevertheless, Robert Frei, with the assistance of his new vice-president, artist Francis Deck, continued to lead the company that his grandfather had founded. In 1972 the South Grand offices of Emil Frei, Inc., closed and the company moved to 1017 West Adams in Kirkwood, was renamed Emil Frei Associates, Inc., and is today still in operation.

This history of the Emil Frei Glass Company was written in 1986 by Martha Ramsey Clevenger, Manuscript Processor for the Missouri Historical Society Division of Library and Archives. Thanks to Steven Frei for providing the manuscript for this publication.

APPENDIX 1 DENOMINATIONS

Adventists, Seventh Day

The largest single Adventist body throughout the world is the Seventh Day Adventist Church. The group traces its beginnings back to the 1840's. They trace their convictions on the sabbath back to earlier Seventh Day Baptist of New England and Europe.

Doctrinally, the Seventh Day Adventists are evangelical conservatives. Their standard statement of belief reveals that they take the Bible as their sole rule of faith and practice; that they believe in God as revealed in the Father, the Son and the Holy Spirit, each equally and uniquely divine, personal and eternal. They believe in creation by divine fiat and in the fall of man. Man is saved solely by grace and redeemed only through the atoning death of Jesus Christ.

They hold the Ten Commandments as the standard of righteousness and they base their observance of the seventh day as the sabbath on the Fourth Commandment. They tithe their incomes and support the church solely by this system.

Baptists

The Baptists make up one of the major protestant groups in the United States. Twenty seven Baptist denominations have a membership of over 20,000,000. There are almost 100,000 local Baptist churches, each one independent of the others, with members also independent of one another.

It is often heard that Baptists have no founder but Christ and that Baptists have been preaching and practicing from the days of John the Baptist. As an organized church, Baptists began in Holland and England. The first Protestant Missionary Board in America was made up of Baptists, Reformed, Congregational and Presbyterian churchmen. In 1814 the Baptists organized their own separate General Missionary Convention of the Baptist Denomination in the United States.

The great division over slavery came in 1845, when the Southerners split to form their own Southern Baptist Convention. From then on, there was to be a Northern and a Southern Baptist Convention.

Baptists generally agree on the following principles of faith: The Bible is the sole rule of life; the Lordship of Jesus Christ; the freedom of the individual to approach God for himself; The granting of salvation through faith by way of grace and contact with the Holy Spirit. The Baptists also believe in the Lord's Supper and baptism by immersion. Baptists have insisted on freedom of thought and expression in pulpit and pew which has made them one of the most democratic bodies in America. They have also insisted on absolute autonomy of the local congregation.

Christian Churches (Disciples of Christ)

Early nineteenth century revival movements in the United States resulted indirectly in the creation of new communities. One of them was the Disciples of Christ.

The Christian Church was founded by Thomas Campbell, a clergyman of the seeder branch of the Presbyterian Church in Ireland who settled in western Pennsylvania in 1807. Campbell preached that acceptance of the creed should not be a condition of church communion or fellowship. He also advocated closer relations with Christians in other churches. Campbell, and his son Andrew withdrew from the Presbyterian church in 1809 to establish the Christian Association of Washington, Pennsylvania. After about 1830, the followers of Campbell became known as Christians or Disciples of Christ.

The Disciples believe that the Bible is divinely inspired and they accept it as their only rule of faith and life. They urge a simple usage of the New Testament phraseology as the Godhead. They believe that Christ is the Son of God and that the Holy Spirit is at work in the present world.

Church of Christ (Holiness) U.S.A.

C.P. Jones, a Baptist minister in Alabama and Mississippi left the Baptists in 1894 to seek a faith that would make him "one of Wisdom's true sons, and like Abraham, 'A friend of God,'" He called a convention at Jackson, Mississippi and founded a holiness movement which was at first interdenominational. By 1898, it had become a full-fledged denomination.

The church's doctrine emphasizes original sin, Christ's atonement, and his second coming; sacraments include the gift of the Holy Ghost, baptism by immersion, the Lord's Supper and divine healing.

Church of Christ, Scientist

The roots of the Church of Christ, Scientist and Christian Science came from an incident at Lynn, Massachusetts in 1866. Mary Baker Eddy recovered almost instantly from a severe injury after reading in Matthew 9:1-8 the account of Christ's healing of the man sick from palsy. Profoundly religious and a longtime student of mental and spiritual causation, she attributed causation to God and regarded him as divine Mind.

Christian Science is generally described as "a religious teaching and practice based on the words and works of Jesus Christ." Mrs. Eddy wrote SCIENCE AND HEALTH WITH KEY TO THE SCRIPTURES, which, together with the Bible has become the textbook of Christian Science.

In 1892, Mrs. Eddy established the First Church of Christ, Scientist, in Boston, Massachusetts and its branch churches and societies. That church is known as "The Mother Church. "Christian Science beliefs start with the conviction that God is the only might or Mind; he is "all in All," the "divine principle of all that really is."

Church of God

There are at least 200 different independent religious groups in the United States that call themselves Church of God. Three of these have their headquarters in Cleveland, Tennessee, where the name was first used in the later years of the nineteenth century.

The Cleveland bodies were formed on August 19, 1886 as a Christian fellowship known first as the Christian Union and were led by Richard G. Spurling. In May of 1902, the Union was reorganized under the name of "The Holiness Church." A.J. Tomlinson, an America Bible Society colporteur, joined them in 1903 and was elected general overseer in 1909. He was impeached in 1923 and at that time started his own group known as the Tomlinson Church of God. In 1953, the name was changed to the Church of God in Prophecy. When Tomlinson died in 1943, one of his sons organized his followers under the name Church of God in Queens, New York.

Another body known as the original Church of God was organized in 1917 following a split with the followers of Richard G. Spurling. It is headquartered in Chattanooga, Tennessee.

Church of God in Christ

C.H. Mason and C.P. Jones left the Baptist groups in Arkansas for considered overemphasis in Holiness and founded the Church of God in Christ in 1887. Mason put strong emphasis on entire sanctification and in a revival received the baptism of the Holy Spirit together with signs of "speaking with tongues."

Churches of Christ

Twenty thousand independent congregations make up the Churches of Christ. They are located in all 50 states and 65 foreign countries. The Churches of Christ have become one of the top ten non-Catholic bodies in North America.

The churches have roots in the movements which inspired the founding of the Christian Church and the Disciples of Christ. Those who founded the Church of Christ were originally members of the Disciples of Christ but were a conservative group who conflicted with the more progressive Disciples over questions of pastoral power and the use of the title Reverend instead of Elder.

One of the significant features of the Churches of Christ is in their acceptance of the Bible as a true and completely adequate revelation.

Churches of God, Holiness

The Churches of God, Holiness, began in 1914 with a group of 8 people in Atlanta, Georgia, under the preaching of K.H. Burrus. Large churches were founded in Atlanta and in

Norfolk, Virginia., in 1916. By 1922, these churches were incorporated into what is currently known as the National Convention of the Churches of God, Holiness.

All Doctrine within this group is tested by strict New Testament standards; the Scriptures are accepted as inspired, and the New Testament gives clearly applied instructions on all methods of labor, sacred and secular. These instructions are clearly applied on the conduct of the whole of life. The churches believe in the Trinity, in justification, entire sanctification and that the gift of the Holy Spirit is an act subsequent to conversion.

EASTERN ORTHODOX CHURCHES

The most important split in the history of Christianity came about in A.D. 330 when Constantine moved his capital from Rome to Byzantium and began to rule from Constantinople. Conflict deepened between the pope and the patriarch at Constantinople. The Eastern Church held that the Holy Spirit proceeded directly from the Father; the Western Church had adopted the view that the Spirit proceeded from the Father and the Son. In 1054, the pope excommunicated the patriarch and the patriarch excommunicated the pope. The result of this was that there were finally two churches. The pope remained the head of the Western Church. In the East, there were four patriarchs or heads guiding the destinies of Eastern Orthodoxy. It is not a monarchy like the Western Church, but is based on the body of bishops. Today, Christendom remains divided into three principal sections: Roman Catholic, Eastern Orthodox and Protestant.

Greek Orthodox

The Greeks arriving in the United States in the early part of the twentieth century asked for and secured the services of Orthodox priests sent to them by the Holy Synod of Greece or the Ecumenical Patriarchate of Constantinople. In 1922, an act known as The Founding Tome of 1922 established the Greek Orthodox Archdiocese of North and South America.

Doctrine and policy are of the usual Eastern Orthodox patterns.

Russian Orthodox Church

Eastern Orthodoxy came to Russia with the baptism of Vladimir in A.D. 988. Government of the church was at first in the hands of people appointed by the patriarch of Constantinople. A Holy Synod was instituted during the reign of Peter the Great. From 1721 to 1917 the Holy Synod was made up of 3 metropolitans and other bishops from various parts of Russia.

Eight Russian Orthodox monks established headquarters at Kodiak Alaska in 1792 and built there the first Eastern Orthodox Church in America. A chapel was built at a Russian trading post near present day San Francisco and in 1872, and an episcopal was established in that city. In 1905, the Russian episcopal was moved to New York City.

Serbian Eastern Orthodox Church

The Church in Serbia from the seventh century to the thirteenth was under the jurisdiction of the greek patriarchate of Constantinople and became the independent National Serbian Church in 1219. Serbian immigrants began to arrive in great numbers in the United States about 1890. They worshipped first at Russian churches until they sent their first bishop in 1926. Headquarters were established at St. Sava's Serbian Monastery at Libertyville, Illinois.

Eastern Rite Churches

The Eastern Rite churches are communities of eastern Christians in union with the Roman Catholic Church. They maintain distinctive spiritual, liturgical and canonical traditions. Some of them also permit a married clergy.

The five major divisions of the Eastern Rite or Uniate churches are the Alexandrian, Antiochene, Armenian, Chaldean and Byzantine. These churches generally originated under the political influence of the Roman Catholic Church. The largest eastern Rite church is the Ukrainian Catholic Church which was formed when Ukrainian subjects of the king of Poland were united with Rome in 1596. Another large group are the Maronites of Lebanon which was established when their country was occupied by Western Crusaders in the 12th century.

Each Eastern Rite church is headed by a patriarch who has jurisdiction over the bishops, clergy and people of that rite. All of the patriarchs are members of the Congregation for the Oriental Churches, which governs the relations of the Vatican with the Eastern Rites.

Evangelical Congregational Church

The Evangelical Church withdrew from the Evangelical Association in 1894 to organize the United Evangelical Church. The two churches were reunited in 1922, but again a minority objected and remained aloof from the merger. The East Pennsylvania Conference, along with several churches in the Central, Pittsburgh, Ohio and Illinois Conferences continued their separate existence. This group later changed their name to the Evangelical Congregational Church.

Judaism

Jews arrived early in the American colonies. Small groups were here before 1650 and by 1657 there was a small group of Jews at Newport, Rhode Island. In 1733, a Jewish synagogue was organized at Savannah, Georgia. By 1850 there were 77 Jewish congregations in 21 states and at the end of the century, more than 600 congregations.

Judaism is the oldest living religion in the Western world. Historically, Judaism serves as the matrix for Christianity and Islam. Judaism was the first religion to teach Monotheism, or belief in one God. Jews believe that God's providence extends to all people but that God entered into a special covenant with the ancient Israelites.

The two pillars upon which Judaism rests. One is the teaching of the Old Testament, especially the five books of Moses. This is known in Judaism as the Torah or the Pentateuch. It is the revelation of God, divine in origin and containing the earliest written laws and traditions of the Jewish people. The other is the Talmud, which is a rabbinical commentary and enlargement of the Torah, an elaborate compendium containing the written and oral law which guides the Jew in every phase of his life.

In Torah and Talmud are the Judaistic foundation principles of justice, purity, hope, thanksgiving, righteousness, love, freedom of will, divine providence and human responsibility, repentance, prayer and the resurrection of the dead.

The Sabbath, from sunset Friday to sunset Saturday, is observed by refraining from work and by attending a synagogue service. In accordance with biblical law, men wear a fringed shawl or tallith during prayer and covering the head is a widespread custom.

Judaism looks forward to the perfection of man and to the establishment of a perfect divine kingdom of truth and righteousness.

There are 4 divisions in American Judaism: Orthodox, Reform, Conservative and Reconstruction. The first three of these national organizations are members of the Synagogue Council of America.

Lutherans

Lutheran was a name attached to the followers of Martin Luther by their enemies in the time of the Protestant Reformation. Luther's position was that the Catholic Church and papacy had no divine right in things spiritual, that the scriptures and not the Roman Catholic priest or church had final authority over conscience. Luther said that Men were forgiven and absolved of their sins not by good works or by imposition of church rite, but by man's Holy Spirit empowered action in turning from sin directly to God. Justification came through faith and not through ceremony.

The Reformation resulted not in a united Protestantism, but in a Protestantism with 2 branches: Evangelical Lutheranism, led by Luther and the Reformed Church led by Calvin. Evangelical Lutheranism spread from Germany to Poland, Russia, Lithuania, France and Holland and others. It was mainly from Germany and Scandinavia that Lutheranism came to the United States. The first European Lutherans arrived in the United States from Holland in 1623. The first independent group of Lutherans was established in New Sweden along the Delaware in 1638. The German Lutherans who settled in New York were mostly exiles from Salzburg who also settled in Georgia. The greatest influx of Lutherans settled in Pennsylvania where by the Middle 18th century there were 30,000, mostly German.

The need for organization resulted in the creation of the General Synod in 1820. After westward expansion extended Lutheranism, the Missouri Synod was formed in 1847 and the German Iowa Synod formed in 1854. By 1870, the Lutherans were the fourth largest Protestant group in the United States with about 400,000 members. Today, the Lutheran Church Missouri Synod is the second largest Lutheran Church in the United States with more than 2,500,000 members.

All Lutheran faith is built on Luther's principle of justification by faith alone in Jesus Christ; the gospel for fallen men. Lutherans believe that the Bible is the inspired word of God and the rule and standard of faith and practice. Lutherans confess their faith through the three general creeds of Christendom, the Apostles', the Nicene and the Athansian. The two sacraments of baptism and the Lord's Supper are channels through which God bestows his forgiving and empowering grace upon men. Infants are baptized and baptized persons are believed to receive the gift of regeneration from the Holy Ghost.

The congregation is the basic unit of Lutheran Government and they are united in Synods composed of pastors and lay representatives elected by the congregations.

In 1961, the American Lutheran Church, Evangelical Lutheran Church and the United Evangelical Lutheran Church were merged into the American Lutheran Church. Later, the United Lutheran Church of America, the American Evangelical Lutheran, the Finnish Evangelical Lutheran and the Augustana Evangelical Lutheran Church combined under the name Lutheran Church in America.

Methodists

Methodism is a name given to a group of Protestant churches that arose from the 18th century Wesleyan movement in England led by John and Charles Wesley and George Whitefield. Originally centered in Great Britain and North America, Methodism has spread worldwide. The world Methodist community is estimated to be more than 38 million; the largest group being the United Methodist Church in the United States.

In 1738, the Wesleys organized small societies within the Church of England for religious sharing, Bible study, prayer and teaching. The Methodist doctrine was based on an Arminian interpretation of the Thirty Nine Articles but emphasized personal experience of conversion, assurance and sanctification.

George Whitefield conducted preaching tours in North America and was a significant influence in the Great Awakening. Wesleyan Methodism was later established in America by unofficial lay missionaries such as Philip Embury and others along with appointed missionaries sent by John Wesley such as Francis Asbury. In 1874, Thomas Coke was appointed the superintendent for America and led to the organization of the Methodist Episcopal Church in Baltimore.

In 1830, due to a controversy over episcopal authority, the Methodist Protestant Church was formed by a liberal minority. In 1843, the wesleyan Methodist Church of America was started by a group of antislavery Methodists. The following year the General Conference split over slavery issues and episcopal authority and the Methodist Episcopal Church, South, was formed at the Louisville convention in 1845. In 1860, the antislavery Free Methodist Church was formed. Later, three black churches were also organized in protest against racial prejudice: The African Methodist Episcopal in 1816, the African Methodist Episcopal Zion in 1820 and the Colored (later Christian) Methodist Episcopal Church in 1870.

When the Northern and Southern branches and the Methodist Protestants united in 1939, a reunion was achieved. In 1968, that church merged with the Evangelical United Brethren Church to form the United Methodist Church.

Mormons (Church of Jesus Christ of Latter Day Saints)

Although no historic Mormon churches are evident in the St. Louis area, the roots and history of this group is prominent.

Mormonism is a way of life practiced by members of the Church of Jesus Christ of Latter Day Saints. Although two-thirds of the church's membership is in the United States, members are also found in 100 other countries and 25 territories, colonies and possessions. The Mormons have a worldwide membership of about 7 million.

Joseph Smith founded the Mormon Church in Fayetteville, North Carolina in 1830. Smith reported that he had experienced visions of God and other heavenly beings in which he was told that he would be the instrument of establishing the restored Christian church. Smith said that one of the heavenly messengers directed him to some thin metal gold plates which were inscribed with a hieroglyphic language. Smith translated the plates into the Book of Mormon, which describes the history, wars, and religious beliefs of a group of people from around 600 B.C. who migrated to America from Jerusalem.

Smith attracted a small group of followers who settled in Kirkland, Ohio and Jackson, Missouri Because of persecution the church moved to northern Missouri and then to Nauvoo, Illinois. The church prospered in Nauvoo, but neighbors became upset when rumors spread that Smith had secretly introduced polygamy into Mormonism. On June 2, 1844, an armed mob killed Smith, who had been jailed in Carthage, Illinois. Brigham Young, was voted the new leader of the church on August 8, 1844 and in 1846, he organized and directed the epic move from Nauvoo to the Great Salt Lake area.

The church continued to grow in Utah, but it was challenged by the United States government because of the acceptance of polygamy as a Mormon tenet. After much fighting, Mormon leaders compromised. In 1862 and 1882, Congress passed antibigamy laws, and in 1879, the Supreme Court rules that religious freedom could not be claimed as grounds for the practice of polygamy. The practice was officially ended in 1890.

Not all Mormons supported Young's election as church leader. The opposition withdrew to form other churches. The largest of these is the Reorganized Church of Jesus Christ of Latter Day Saints, which is headquartered at Independence, Missouri. This church holds that rightful leadership belongs only to the descendants of Joseph Smith.

Mormons use the Bible, the Book of Mormon and two other revelations to Joseph Smith as their standard scriptures. Because of this, they share most of the beliefs of traditional Christianity with some modification. Mormons

believe that God still reveals his word to individuals who seek it for their benefit and to church leaders who use this revelation for the church.

Mormons baptize by immersion at age eight or older. Vicarious baptism for those who have died and marriage for eternity are two distinctive Mormon beliefs. The church lays great emphasis on genealogical research so that members may undergo baptismal rites on behalf of their ancestors. Church members tithe to support church activities. Members operate the full program for each congregation. The church places great emphasis on family solidarity, encouraged through a weekly family evening of religious instruction and entertainment.

Pentecostal Bodies

Many Pentecostal churches have come from Methodist or Baptist backgrounds and are primarily concerned with perfection, holiness and the Pentecostal experience.

Most Pentecosts believe in the trinity, original sin, man's salvation through the atoning blood of Christ, the virgin birth and the deity of Jesus. They also believe in the literal infallibility of the Bible, manifestations and blessings of the Holy Spirit running into excessive emotionalism such as shouting, trances, jerking, hand clapping and tongue talking. Two sacraments are found in most sects; baptism by immersion and the Lord's Supper.

Pentecosts are found in every state with the greatest strength in the South, West and Midwest. The majority of American Pentecosts may be found in the Tomlinson groups of the Church of God and related groups. Pentecost churches include: the Church of God in Christ (Pentecostal), Pentecostal Assemblies, The Pentecostal Church of Christ and the United Pentecostal Church.

Presbyterians

The word Presbyterianism refers to the form of church government in which elders, both lay and ministers govern. The name derives from the Greek word presbuteros, or "elder." There are approximately 50 million Protestants around the world that practice Presbyterian church government. Large numbers of Presbyterians are to be found in Scotland, Northern Ireland, England, the Netherlands, Switzerland, France and others. The largest Presbyterian body is the Presbyterian Church (U.S.A), with 3 million members. This group was formed in 1983 by the union of the United Presbyterian Church and the (Southern) Presbyterian Church in the United States. There are other Presbyterian and Reformed denominations in the United States that trace their origins to Europe or to secessions from the larger American bodies. The older name Reform Churches remains prevalent among groups of continental European origin while Presbyterian is generally used by churches of British origin.

The Presbyterian movement emerged during the 16th century Reformation as an effort by Protestant reformers to recapture the form as well as the message of the New Testament church. John Calvin, the Swiss Reformed leader, concluded that Jesus Christ himself is the sole ruler of the church and that he exercises this rule through four kinds of people: preachers, teachers, deacons and lay elders.

Calvin's Genevan church order was carried to Scotland by John Knox and evolved into the Presbyterianism that is still practiced today. Individual congregations elect their elders including the minister. Presbyteries select delegates to regional synods which in turn select representatives to the General Synod, a national body.

The Westminster Assembly in 1643-49 produced the doctrinal and ecclesiastical standards that are the foundation for Presbyterians. Presbyterian worship is simple and orderly and revolves around preaching from the Bible. Two sacraments are recognized: the Lord's Supper and baptism, which is administered to the infant children.

Protestant Episcopal Church

The Protestant Episcopal Church in the United States is part of the worldwide Anglican Communion. In the late 1980's the church had about 2, 500,000 members in about 7,000 parishes and missions.

The Episcopal church began with the English exploration and colonization of North America. Although the New England colonies were established by Puritans who were opposed to Anglicanism, large numbers of Anglicans settled in the southern colonies, and the Church of England became the established church. In 1789, the Protestant Episcopal Church began its separate existence. This group's beliefs were based not only on its Anglican heritage, but a commitment to such American ideals as the separation of Church and State. The Protestant Episcopal Church constitutes the self-governing branch of the Anglican Communion. For its first 150 years, it bore the name of the Church of England. This became the established church in the south.

Roman Catholic

The Roman Catholic Church is the largest of the Christian churches. It is identified as Roman because of its historical roots in Rome and because of the importance it places in the worldwide ministry of the bishop of Rome, the pope.

In 1980 there were over 780 million Roman Catholics in the world, with over 51 million in the United States.

The basic beliefs of Roman Catholics are those shared by other Christians as derived from the New Testament. The central belief is that God entered the world through the incarnation of his Son, Jesus Christ. The founding of the church is traced to the life and teachings of Jesus, whose death is followed by resurrection from the dead after which he sends the Holy Spirit to assist believers. The triple mission within the Godhead is known as the divine Trinity, God in one nature but existing in three divine persons.

The beginnings of the church date from the moment of Christ's selection of the apostle Peter as guardian of the keys of heaven and earth and as chief of the apostles. The Catholic Church claims Peter as its first pope. The church gained power when it arose as the only body strong enough to rule after the fall of Rome in 410 A.D. The first mention of the word Catholic, which means "universal" was made by Ignatius about 110-15 A.D.

Roman Catholics place special significance to the rites of Baptism, which is sacramental entry into Christian life, and the Eucharist which is a memorial of Christ's death and resurrection. The Eucharist is celebrated daily in the Roman Catholic Church. Catholics also regard as sacraments the confession, the Holy Orders, Marriage of Christians, confirmation and the annoiting of the sick.

Catholic ethical doctrines are based not only on the New Testament but also on the conclusions reached by the church. The pope and bishops have formulated guidelines regarding social justice, racial equality, contraception and abortion. The Roman Catholic prohibition of marriage after divorce is the strictest of all Christian churches.

The public worship of the Roman Catholic Church is called the Mass. After the prayers and Bible readings, the priest invites the congregation to receive communion. At the Sunday liturgy the priest preaches a sermon or homily. In addition to the normal Christian holidays, the Roman Catholic Church also commemorates the saints. A distinguishing mark of Catholic worship is prayer for the dead. The devotional importance attached to the saints distinguishes the Roman Catholic Church from the churches of the reformation.

The Roman Catholic Church is organized locally into neighborhood parishes and regional dioceses administered by bishops. Catholic Church policy is led by a centralized government under the pope. The pope is elected for life by the College of Cardinals. He is assisted in the governing of the church by the bishops. The Roman Catholic Church has a tradition of all-male ordained clergy. In the Western Rite Catholic Church, bishops and priests are celibate.

Some Catholics live together in religious orders, serving the church and the world under vows of poverty, chastity and obedience. Members of these orders include sisters, (nuns), brothers and priests.

United Church of Christ

The United Church of Christ was established in 1957 as a union of the Congregational Christian Churches and the Evangelical and Reformed Church. The Congregational and Christian Churches were merged first in 1931 and then were joined by the Evangelical and Reformed in 1957. With a current membership of about 1.7 million, the United Church of Christ is the youngest of the major Protestant denominations in the United States. The roots of the United Church of Christ lie in the teachings of the 16th century reformer such as Martin Luther and Ulrich Zwingli and in Congregationalism.

The basic unit of the United Church is the local church, which has autonomy, or freedom in the decisions it makes. That freedom is the freedom of the gospel and every corporate body within the church is supposed to make its decisions in the light of the gospel and out of a sense of responsibility to the whole fellowship.

The General Synod of the United Church of Christ is the representative, deliberative body composed of delegates elected by conferences. The United Church of Christ is a member of the National Council of Churches, the World Council of Churches and the World Alliance of Reformed Churches.

Unitarian Universalist Association

The Unitarian Universalist Association was founded in 1961 by consolidation of the American Unitarian Association (1825) and the Universalist Church of America (1793). The church headquarters is in Boston where it carries on common activities such as ministerial settlement and preparation of educational materials, but it does not exercise hierarchical control. The church's philosophy is one of religious liberalism, stressing the value of human freedom and rejecting dogmatic formulations. The denomination is connected with other similar groups around the world through the International Association for Religious Freedom. The church has about 145,250 adult members in more than 1000 churches in North America.

Unitarianism is a form of Christianity that asserts that God is one person, the father, rather than three persons in one as the doctrine of the Trinity holds. Another significant belief is their confidence in the reasoning and moral abilities of people in contrast to traditions that emphasize original sin and human depravity. Unitarianism appeared in the United States around 1740-43.

GLOSSARY

Ambulatory   Aisle around the chancel used for processions.

Aisle   Side areas running parallel to the nave.

Altar   Table or stone slab on supports used for celebration of the Eucharist.

Arcade   Range of arches carried on columns or piers.

Arch   Structural support between two columns or piers made in an inverted curve.

Archbishop   A bishop of high rank.

Archdiocese   The diocese of an Archbishop.

Archiepiscopal   Of or relating to an Archbishop.

Basilica   Early style of church consisting of a nave and two or more lower, narrower aisles. Also, a church or cathedral given ceremonial privileges.

Bay   Section of wall between pillars. A nave consists of a succession of bays.

Berma   Raised platform in early churches, on which the preacher stood to speak.

Baptism   Baptism is a vivid visual demonstration of becoming a Christian.

Baptistery   Building or section of the church used for baptism.

Bishop   A clergyman ranking above a priest and typically governing a diocese.

Boss   Ornamental knob covering the intersection of ribs in a vault or ceiling.

Buttress   Brick or stonework built against a wall to give it support.

Byzantine   The style of architecture introduced at Byzantium in the fifth century. It is derived from the Roman but distinguished from it by the general use of the dome or cupola.

Capital   Top crowning feature of a column or pier.

Cathedral   The principal church of a diocese.

Chancel   Eastern end of a church sometimes reserved for the clergy and choir.

Chapel   Any building or part of a building enclosing an alter and intended in some measure for private worship.

Chevron   Romanesque decoration in the form of a zig-zag.

Choir   Area of the church where the services are sung. The area occupied by the singers.

Church   In Christian theology, the church is the community of those who are called to acknowledge Jesus Christ. Church also designates the building used for Christian worship.

Clerestory   Upper level of the nave wall, pierced by windows.

Cloisters   External quadrangle surrounded by a covered walkway.

Column   Vertical load bearing shaft with circular cross-section.

Communion   A Christian sacrament in which bread and wine are partaken as a commemoration of the death of Christ.

Congregation   An assembly of persons met especially for worship.   A company or order of religious persons under a common rule.

Cornice   Topmost decorative molded section surmounting a column. Also any projecting molding at the roof level of a building.

Crossing   The intersection of the nave and the transept, the crossing is a natural center for a church.

Crypt   Space beneath the main floor of a church.

Denomination   A religious body comprising a number of local congregations having a similar belief.

Dome   Vault built on a circular base.

Diocese   The territorial jurisdiction of a bishop.

Entablature   Uppermost part of the order surrounding a column. Consists of cornice, frieze and architrave.

Facing   Finish material applied to the outside of a building.

Fascia   A broad fillet, band or face used in Classical architecture.

Finial   Ornament at the tip of a spire, pinnacle or canopy.

Flying Buttress   Buttress in the form of an arch, supporting the upper portion of a wall.

Gallery   Upper story inside of a church, above the aisle, open to the nave.

Gargoyle   Water spout projecting from a roof, often carved as a head or figure.

Gothic   A style of architecture prevalent in western Europe from the middle 12th to the early 16th century.   Gothic architecture is characterized by the buttress, the flying buttress, the pointed arch and the ribbed vault. Traceries are used to divide large windows and there is a preference for vertical rather than horizontal lines.

Greek Cross   A Style of architecture used for many Eastern church which represents the cross with four arms of equal length.

Grisalle   Stained glass with mostly white glass in small lozenge-shaped panes painted in decorative patterns.

Groin Angle formed by intersection of vaults.

Hall Church Church in which nave and aisles are about the same height.

Icon Image of a saint, apostle or martyr used as an aid for worship of God especially in Eastern churches.

Keystone Central stone in an arch or rib.

Lantern Circular or polygonal tower topping a dome or roof.

Lectern Desk or stand on which books are placed.

Lights Openings between the mullions of a window.

Lintel Horizontal timber or stone beam.

Lombard A style of architecture developed in Lombardy in Italy characterized by the frequent use of the groined vault, and the buildings are somberly impressive due to heavy proportions and details. The exteriors use plain walls of brick or stone reinforced by buttress strips.

Moldings Contoured shaping given to projecting elements such as arches, lintels, string courses, etc.

Mullion Wooden or stone framework within a window.

Narthex Vestibule across the west end of a church.

Nave Main middle section of the inside of a church running from the west end to the crossing.

Order A combination of columns, base, capitals and entablature developed in ancient Rome and Greece and extensively copied in periods of classical revival. The most usual orders are Doric, Ionic, and Corinthian.

Pew Benches on which to sit in a church or cathedral.

Pier Solid vertical masonry support with non circular cross-section.

Pilaster Shallow pier or squared column attached to a wall.

Pinnacle Small tower-like top to a spire or buttress.

Presbytery The part of the church in which the high altar is placed.

Priest A person having the authority to perform the sacred rites of a religion.

Pulpit A raised platform or reading desk used in preaching or conducting a worship service.

Rabbi Master, teacher. A Jew trained and ordained for religious leadership.

Renaissance A style of architecture which draws its inspiration from classical forms. Church plans are generally more compact than Gothic style. French Gothic styles.

Rib Projecting stone or brickwork on a ceiling or vault, usually load-bearing.

Romanesque A style of architecture in which the mass of the wall is heavy and often decorated with frescoes. An outstanding achievement of Romanesque architecture is the development of stone vaulted buildings. Features include barrel vaults, ribbed groin vaults and domes. Massiveness in stone structures is a major characteristic of Romanesque architecture.

Sanctuary Area around the communion table on the east end of a church.

Shrine A repository for relics.

Spire Tall conical or polygonal structure built on top of a tower.

Stained Glass Translucent colored or tinted glass used in churches and cathedrals

Steeple Combination of tower and spire.

String Course Projecting molded horizontal band of stonework.

Synagogue The house of worship of a Jewish congregation.

Tabernacle Ornamental receptacle or recess to contain relics or the sacraments used in the Eucharist.

Temple An edifice for the worship of a deity. Also, a place devoted to a special or exalted purpose.

Tower A tower extends the range from which a church is visible and is used to support bells.

Tracery Ornamental shaped stone or woodwork in windows or screens.

Transept Reverse arms of a cross-shaped church. Projects at right angles from the body.

Triforium Middle level of nave between the arcade and clerestory. A gallery or arcade in the wall over the arches.

Tudor Style Identified with perpendicular work in long suites as a crest, or ornamental finishing on cornices.

Tympanum Area between the lintel of a doorway and the arch above it.

Vault Arched ceiling. There are several types of vault. They are the barrel vault, the groin vault, the lierne vault and the quadripartite vault.

Vestibule A hall or ante-chamber next to the entrance from which doors open to the various rooms or passages of a house.

Vestry A room attached to the choir of a church.

This map gives an illustration of the distribution of historic churches in St. Louis County and surrounding areas. See the address on the individual church pages for an exact location. See the map on the following page for distribution of churches in the city of St. Louis.

Distribution of historic churches in the city of St. Louis. See the address on the individual church pages for an exact location.

Map of St. Louis city neighborhoods used with permission of the St. Louis Regional Commerce and Growth Association.

Selected Bibliography

Archdiocesan Council of the Laity. *Historic Churches in St. Louis*, St. Louis, Missouri, 1976.

Broderick, Robert C. *Historic Churches of the United States*, New York, NY: Wilfred Funk, Inc., 1958

Brown, Jo Ann. *St. Charles Borromeo-200 years of Faith*, St. Louis, Missouri: The Patrice Press, 1991.

Clowney, Paul & Tessa. *Exploring Churches*, Grand Rapids, Michigan: William E. Eerdmans Publishing Co., 1982

Faherty, S.J., William Barnaby. *Dream By the River*, St. Louis, Missouri: River City Publishers, 1981.

Faherty, S.J., William Barnaby. *The St. Louis Portrait*, Tulsa, Oklahoma: Continental Heritage, Inc. 1978.

Faherty, S.J., William Barnaby. *St. Louis-A Concise History*, St. Louis, Missouri: The Masonry Institute of St. Louis. 1989

Franzwa, Gregory. *The Old Cathedral*, St. Louis, Missouri: The Patrice Press.

Hagen, Harry M. *This is our St. Louis*, St. Louis, Missouri: Knight Publishing Co., 1970.

Hannon, Robert E. *St. Louis: Its Neighborhoods, Neighbors, Landmarks & Milestones*, St. Louis, Missouri: Regional Commerce and Growth Association, 1986.

Harris, Nini. *A Grand Heritage*. St. Louis, Missouri: DeSales Community Housing Corp. 1984.

Harris, Nini. *A History of Carondelet*. St. Louis, Missouri: The Patrice Press, 1991.

Harris, Nini. *Legacy of Lions*. University City, Missouri: The Historical Society of University City, 1981

Jacob, Robert. *Religions In St. Louis*, St. Louis, Missouri: Interfaith Clergy Council, 1976.

Toft, Carolyn Hughes. *St. Louis: Landmarks & Historic Districts*, St. Louis, Missouri: Landmarks Association of St. Louis, Inc., 1988.

Linderer, Nanette. *St. Louis Churches*, St. Louis, Missouri, 1973.

McCarthy, Marilyn A. *Stones of Remembrance*, Clayton, Missouri: Central Presbyterian Church, 1994

McCue, George & Peters, Frank. *A Guide to the Architecture of St. Louis*, Columbia, Missouri: University of Missouri Press, 1989.

Mead, Frank S. *Handbook of Denominations in the U.S.*, New York, NY: Abington Press, 1961.

St. Ferdinand's Parish, *Dedication Book 1789-1961*, Florissant, Missouri, 1961.

St. Louis County Dept of Parks & Rec., *100 Historic Buildings in St. Louis County*, St. Louis, Missouri, 1970.

St. Nicholas Greek Orthodox Church, *Seventy-Fifth Anniversary Album*, St. Louis, Missouri, 1992.

Seaton, Richard A. *History of the United Methodist Churches of Missouri*, St. Louis, Missouri: Missouri Methodist Historical Society, 1984.

Thornton A.M., Francis A. *The Notable Catholic Institutions of St. Louis & Vicinity*, St. Louis, Missouri: Finkenbiner-Reid Publishing Co., 1911.

Wayman, Norbury L. *History of St. Louis Neighborhoods*, St. Louis, Missouri: St. Louis Community Development Agency.

OTHER BOOKS FROM THE AUTO REVIEW

FOR GARRY OWEN IN GLORY   The true account of an airmobile combat platoon leader with the Seventh Cavalry in Vietnam 1968-69. LTC James J. Schild. 200 Pages, 112 B & W photographs ISBN 0-9624958-0-8

FOUR WHEELS NO BRAKES   The history of the automobile business in St. Louis. Reprint of 1930 edition with 86 pre-1910 stories. 320 pages, 32 B & W photographs ISBN 0-9624958-1-6

EXERCISE EDUCATION   Personal wellness and weight control. Professor Myrna M. Schild. 112 pages, Illustrated. ISBN 0-9624958-2-4

RESTORER'S CLASSIC CAR SHOP
MANUAL   The first real restoration and maintenance guide for the pre-war collector car. The best book of its kind. Jim Schild. 336 pages, 700 illustrations. ISBN 0-9624958-4-0

AA TRUCK SUPPLEMENT TO
RESTORER'S MODEL A SHOP
MANUAL   The long-awaited supplement to the popular Restorer's Model A Shop Manual. Everything for the big iron. Jim Schild. 96 pages, 200 illustrations. ISBN 0-9624958-5-9

Books may be ordered and prices and information requested from: The Auto Review, P.O. Box 510, Florissant, MO 63032 USA

ALSO BY THE AUTHOR

RESTORER'S MODEL A SHOP
MANUAL   The top selling Model A Ford book for more than ten years. The most accurate, complete and well-illustrated restoration and maintenance manual available for the Model A Ford. Jim Schild. 224 pages, 200 photos and illustrations. ISBN 0-87938-194-9 Published by Motorbooks International, Osceola, Wisconsin, 54020.

8 X 10 inch color prints are available of most of the churches featured in HOUSE OF GOD for $10.00 plus $1.50 postage & handling. Send check for $11.50 and indicate which church is desired to The Auto Review, P.O. Box 510, Florissant, MO 63032. (Price subject to change without notice)

Individualized tours of the historic churches of the St. Louis area may be organized by calling Antique Classic Limousine Service at 314-355-3609